Cambridge Elements

Elements in Creativity and Imagination
edited by
Anna Abraham
University of Georgia, USA

LANDSCAPES OF THE IMAGINATION

Gerald C. Cupchik
University of Toronto Scarborough

Shaftesbury Road, Cambridge CB2 8EA, United Kingdom

One Liberty Plaza, 20th Floor, New York, NY 10006, USA

477 Williamstown Road, Port Melbourne, VIC 3207, Australia

314–321, 3rd Floor, Plot 3, Splendor Forum, Jasola District Centre, New Delhi – 110025, India

103 Penang Road, #05–06/07, Visioncrest Commercial, Singapore 238467

Cambridge University Press is part of Cambridge University Press & Assessment, a department of the University of Cambridge.

We share the University's mission to contribute to society through the pursuit of education, learning and research at the highest international levels of excellence.

www.cambridge.org
Information on this title: www.cambridge.org/9781009472050

DOI: 10.1017/9781009472043

When citing this work, please include a reference to the DOI 10.1017/9781009472043

First published 2024

A catalogue record for this publication is available from the British Library

ISBN 978-1-009-47205-0 Hardback
ISBN 978-1-009-47207-4 Paperback
ISSN 2752-3950 (online)
ISSN 2752-3942 (print)

Landscapes of the Imagination

Elements in Creativity and Imagination

DOI: 10.1017/9781009472043
First published online: December 2024

Gerald C. Cupchik
University of Toronto Scarborough

Author for correspondence: Gerald C. Cupchik, Gerald.cupchik@utoronto.ca

Abstract: The idea that imagination is everywhere in life, and that reality is an illusion, may sound absurd to the concrete mind. This Element will try to convince you that imagination manifests in different "phases," encompassing even the most fundamental ideas about what is real (ontology) and what is true (epistemology). It is present in the contents (e.g., images) and the acts (e.g., fantasy) of the mind. Imagination helps us remove barriers through conscious planning and finds ways to fulfill unconscious desires. The many words related to imagination in the English language are part of a unified web and share a "family resemblance." The first section of this Element deals with imagination in everyday life, the second focuses on aesthetic imagination, and the third discusses scholarly approaches that incorporate both imagination types. The fourth section proposes a unified model integrating the diverse ways that imagination is manifested in our culture.

Keywords: imagination, phase theory, emotion, aesthetics, creativity

ISBNs: 9781009472050 (HB), 9781009472074 (PB), 9781009472043 (OC)
ISSNs: 2752-3950 (online), 2752-3942 (print)

Contents

Introduction: A Phase Theory Approach to Imagination

My search for a phase theory of imagination follows the same path as that applied in *The Aesthetics of Emotion: Up the Down Staircase of the Mind-Body* (Cupchik, 2016). The reference to "phase" theory echoes current ideas in physics in a manner comparable to the way Gestalt psychology was influenced by electromagnetic "fields" in the early twentieth century. But there is no attempt here to gain legitimacy through association with the physical sciences. The "phase theory" concept should be understood as a *generative metaphor* (Danziger, 1990) intended to stimulate fresh ideas. A "phase" theory approach to emotion was meant to encompass complementary processes that appear in different evocative situations. Accordingly, emotional experience is considered plastic so that "affects, feelings and emotions are basic phenomena in-the-world which can be understood as bodily and mental reverberations to challenging or meaningful situations" (Danzinger, 1990, p. 130). The contrast between instrumental (i.e., adaptive) actions in challenging situations and expressive (i.e., embodied) reactions to personally meaningful ones is carried over to theorizing about imagination.

A "phase theory" approach to imagination takes note of the "family resemblance" among diverse words generally associated with the concept (see Figure 1). These words can be more concrete (e.g., image, illusion) or abstract (e.g., fantasy, imaginary) and can also be treated as nouns (image, representation) or as verbs involving actions (hallucinating, dreaming). Phase theory implies that these words are part of a "family" representing diverse aspects of a common underlying process. Different scholarly communities favour particular words that fit within their world-views and interests. Thus, cognitivists talk about concrete and measurable "images," while scholars in the humanities might refer to fanciful "imaginaries." Some words related to imagination (e.g., daydream) are readily understood in everyday language, while others are meaningful to specialized discourse communities (e.g., imaginaries). The notion of "family resemblance," encompassing complementary relations between noun and verb forms of concrete and abstract words in different cultures and across time, provides a firm foundation for a phase-based approach to imagination. The contrasting themes of instrumental (i.e., problem-solving) and expressive (i.e., emotionally embodied) experiences carry over from the emotion book and readily apply to "acts of imagination (Cupchik, 2016)." This Element tries to explain how these diverse words are all interrelated within a unified model.

It is important to keep in mind that *words are not things* and so the concept of "imagination" should be addressed, in a reflective manner, as a kind of process. The semiotician Paul Bouissac has warned about an "ontological trap" wherein we "confuse a hypothetical notion, a heuristic model, a semantic category

Figure 1 Phases of the imagination.

(which depends on a particular language) with an actual observable object in the world endowed with its own ontological presence and opacity."[1] Kurt Danziger (1997), a historian of psychology, has similarly criticized contemporary psychology for treating concepts as if they exist independently from how we think about them. We must always remember that "the categories one meets in psychological texts are discursive categories, not the things themselves" (Danziger, 1997, p. 186). As psychology moved from a rich description of phenomena in the lived world to precise measurement, statistical models replaced meaningful dialogue. This is what is meant by the richness versus precision trade-off. Consequently, "theory" in psychology may refer more to artifacts of laboratory operations than to observable phenomena in the lived world. As we review ideas about imagination, it is important to reflectively balance descriptions of phenomena in the world with concepts tied to experimental operations.

James Mark Baldwin (1861–1934) was an important early contributor to the development of psychology as a discipline (and the first psychology lab at my University of Toronto in 1891). In his review of the history of psychology, Baldwin (1905) described Greek philosophers as skilled and detached observers of the world. This was founded on the experience of a consistent and continuous

[1] Personal e-mail communications May 1, 2014.

inner self that is different from other selves and things that might be observed. According to his approach, empirical psychology in nineteenth-century Germany required individuals to be careful naturalists (i.e., observers) but also skilled positivists who created measurable variables. This leads to a concern about whether we preserve ecological validity, and are faithful to imagination in its different phases, while creating theories and predictive models. Are there particular Western biases regarding matters of ontology (about what is "real") and epistemology (about what is "true") in comparison with a classical Chinese approach to imagination?

Baldwin (1908) made an important theoretical contribution that anticipated "phase theory" by describing complementary relations between everyday and imagination processes. He asked: "What is the relation between "'believe' and 'make-believe"? and concluded that they are in fact complementary: "*Belief motives make-believe and make-believe engenders belief*" (Baldwin, 1908, p. 183). There lies a porous boundary between an "objective, common, confirmable" world of "things . . . to which thought must be correct or true" and an "inner" world wherein "selections, manipulations, constructions seem so free that little limitation of a foreign sort appears" (Baldwin, 1908, p. 181). Accordingly:

> the objective contents . . . may be . . . treated in one . . . of two clearly distinguishable ways. Every such object is either one of knowledge, recognized as part of the actual, the external, the true; or it is one of 'semblance' or make-believe, one to be toyed with . . . to get satisfaction from, to image for personal purposes and selective handling, with some measure of disregard of its exact place and relations in the sphere of the actual. The *actual* and the *imaginative,* the merely known and the usefully or playfully or aesthetically – in short the semblantly or imaginatively – known, this is the one universal and ever-present contrast in meanings for cognition (Baldwin, 1908, p. 182).

This contrast between "instrumental" and "expressive" modes of engagement is central to this Element. "The instrumental meaning is always and everywhere *a re-reading imaginatively, purposively, personally of an actual or truthful meaning,* and the truthful reading is always and everywhere *a re-reading as common, stereotyped, actual of an imaginative personal construction* (p. 183). Accordingly, "*We make-believe in order that we may believe!*" (Baldwin, 1908, p. 184) and, further, "*the imaginative has been instrumental to the actual*" (Baldwin, 1908, p. 185). The point is that everyday thought and imagination are not opposing concepts but, rather, lie on a continuum and this is fundamental to a "phase theory" approach. Baldwin's emphasis on complementarity is familiar to Chinese discourse but alien to a Western framing of ideas in terms of opposites.

Many years ago, Francis Sparshott (1926–2015), the distinguished University of Toronto poet and philosopher, said to me:

> Artists do what artists do.
> Philosophers do what philosophers do.
> And psychologists do what psychologists do.

This implies that, when it comes to imagination, communities of creatives and scholars will have different ways of experiencing and describing the phenomena of interest to them, and this will shape both their experiences and practices. In the midst of this diversity, we will search for a unifying model that accommodates variations or phases. The Element begins with an account of imagination in everyday life (Section 1) and this is followed by an exploration of aesthetic imagination (Section 2). The contrast between everyday instrumental and aesthetic imagination was central to Baldwin's (1908) discussion. Scholarly perspectives on both domains are introduced in Section 3 and an effort is made at a unifying phase-based model in Section 4.

1 Imagination in Everyday Life

What Is Not Imagination, And Does It Exist?

1.1 Dilemmas: Complementary Facets of Imagination

Of perception: You are waiting anxiously for a friend, who is late to arrive, and see someone in the distance who appears familiar. You decide that your friend has finally arrived. As they get closer, you realize that, in fact, this is not the person and cannot believe you made a mistake.

It was in your imagination.

Of emotion: You finally get up the courage to tell someone that you have a deep affection for them. They act surprised and you are embarrassed. You thought they felt the same way.

It was in your imagination.

Of performance: You think your supervisor holds you in great esteem because of a project that you successfully completed. Then you get your annual evaluation and are surprised this seeming success was not acknowledged.

It was in your imagination.

Of memory: You have a distinct recollection of having been somewhere before and can even come up with details about who was there, what you did, and so forth. You bring this up in conversation with friends and they say that, for sure, you were never there.

It was in your imagination.

Of childhood. In your childhood, you had a range of fantasy-based friends that were not "real." They were in your imagination but that was fine.

At work: You come up with a whole new way of solving a problem and your boss really likes it. It came from your imagination but that was great.

Of dreams: You have a dream about falling out of your canoe that quickly recedes into the distance, pushed by the wind, and realize you can't catch up to it even as a strong swimmer. So you swim back to the dock and then your husband appears in his kayak. In the morning, you recall your dream and realize that the episode captured the next phase in your career, with retirement looming. The dream embodies the challenge that you face but clearly you arrived safely at the dock. All will be well.

Relating to your future: COVID has been a crisis for many of us. But, while there are constraints and dangers, there are also opportunities. You imagine a new career path which also gives you a fresh start. This is great.

In relation to your identity: You have always seen yourself in a certain way but have decided to redefine yourself for whatever reason and this is very satisfying. Your imagination gave you a new lease on life.

1.2 Survival and the "Effort after Meaning"

As we can see in these everyday examples, imagination can be deceiving but also lays the foundation for opportunities to be creative. The search for stability and consistency in objects and people in familiar situations is fundamental in everyday life. This begins early in childhood when we learn to manipulate things so as to fulfil needs and desires. The same might be said regarding complex social relationships. We interpret the actions of people in situations, *seeing* them *as* parents or friends, and learn to *see that* by acting in particular ways we can get around obstacles and achieve our goals. Of course, the same principle can be applied to how we see and understand ourselves in a world filled with challenges and opportunities. I would go so far as to argue that *stability is an illusion* in the sense that we create or construct the feeling of stability by integrating, averaging over, all the separate episodes of our lives. Psychologists use the words "images" and "representations" to capture this illusion of stability and concreteness.

There are two sides to our experiences in everyday life that contribute to the illusion of stability. One side involves instrumental actions, related to survival, that enable us to address challenges and fulfill needs or realize goals. The other side involves reactions to situations that are personally meaningful and trigger emotionally tinged memories. In these examples, crisis-like situations may disrupt the smooth flow of actions but also provide an occasion to develop creative strategies and discover new possibilities. Indeed, the Chinese logogram for "crisis" is composed of complementary concepts, "danger" and "opportunity." Resilience reflects an ability to learn from challenging experiences so that we are successful in new situations. The COVID-19 pandemic posed challenges and constraints on people around the world. While some succumbed to "situational helplessness," others were resilient, learned lessons, and redesigned their lives (Cupchik et al., 2024). Erroneous imagination might paralyze us, whereas creative imagination lies at the heart of successful pathways to the future (again, danger and opportunity).

The search for stability in everyday life must balance responses to outside pressures, while at the same time addressing internal needs, wishes, and desires.

Challenges to survival posed by the outside world apply to all living creatures. According to Darwin's "survival of the fittest" principle, "seeing that" acting in such and such a manner will facilitate the realization of goals and, hence, survival. This search for stability, and an effort after meaning, begins with sensory perception and extends to thought, developing into a kind of habit. We learn to identify objects and interpret situations that may vary over time and in different cultures. The rattles in our cribs and the laptops on our desks share something in common; they are both tools either for play or productivity. Grasping and shaking a rattle can happen spontaneously, making it "real." But training is required to use a laptop, especially when a new operating system is introduced. These "schemas" or "representations" serve as a foundation for illusions of stability and continuity in our lives.

My point is that we move quickly and smoothly through our worlds because of familiarity and rehearsal. It bears noting that we can attend an event with friends and yet have very different perspectives literally, because of where we are standing, and metaphorically due to our differential knowledge of the people and relationship to the context. Accordingly, we construct our understanding of situations from the very first moments of perception, given our expectations or needs, and these representations can either be accurate or fraught with error. When we say to someone that "this is in your imagination," we mean that the person has interpreted a situation differently from us, implying that the other person's inferences were inaccurate at best or delusional at worst. Stability represents a kind of illusion or representation, a central tendency that summarizes the individual moments of life. At the same time, internal pressures to fulfil emotional needs, bodily desires, wishes, and plans are often part of internal dialogues, stories that we tell ourselves.

Some situations are clear-cut because of established rules and conventions, such as what happens when we drive a car or play a game of baseball. If we make a mistake while driving, an accident may occur, or the runner is safe at first base because of a throwing error. Matters related to physical survival are easier to identify, compared with backroom politics which might impact our careers and livelihoods. Surprising situations require immediate adjustment so that our actions and goals can continue unimpeded. In the case of a potential traffic accident, we implement well-rehearsed avoidance maneuvers and similar adjustments can take place in games where alternative strategies have been practiced. The novelty of a situation, or ones that are ambiguous, opens the door for "acts of imagination," creative actions which are needed because an initial attempt at categorization or interpretation, and related action, failed.

1.3 Instrumental and Expressive/Embodied Aspects of Imagination

I have described the circumstances *when* imagination is stimulated by events that are either outside the situation or inside the layered history of a person's mind and body. It can be instrumental in the sense of helping us solve unanticipated problems or expressive as an emotional reaction to a story triggered by the unexpected event. This all seems like a roundabout way of addressing a challenging question: *what* exactly is imagination? Here is a preliminary definition. *Imagination is like a web, encompassing sensation, meaning, memory, emotion, and bodily states in a unified experience.* It is not a faculty or thing located at a particular place in our brains. Problems with ambiguous sensations can lead to the experience of *illusions*. Problems with the ambiguous meaning of situations can set the stage for *delusions*, as when one projects incorrect or biased thoughts and interpretations on to the situation. *Hallucinations* represent a more extreme case, as when emotionally loaded meanings distort perception with the attribution of reality to seemingly external characters and stories or events projected onto an ambiguous scene.

1.4 Landscapes of The Imagination

The landscape of imagination comprises both contents and acts that can be applied in the past, present, and future. Contents of the imagination (nouns) encompass all manner of representations, including conjectures, illusions, images, imagery, imaginary associations, and so forth. Acts of imagination (verbs) are embodied or expressive activities that generate these contents, including: fantasying, dreaming, daydreaming, hallucinating, and so forth. In this next section, we examine two dimensions underlying contents and three dimensions onto which processes related to acts of imagination can be mapped.

1.4.1 Contents of Imagination: Two Dimensions

Here is a two-dimensional account of events within the person that are related to different contents of imagination. The contrast, on a horizontal dimension, is between *sensations* versus *actions*, while the vertical dimension contrasts *mind* versus *bodily* dynamics (see Figure 2). On the left pole of the horizontal dimension, we find *sensations* that can be associated with *illusions*, reflecting perceptual errors due to *ambiguity* in the image. This can be contrasted with *motor actions*, on the right pole, guided by possible *misinterpretations* of a situation and manifesting as *hallucinations*, in extreme cases. The vertical dimension contrasts *sentient* or cognitive processes within the brain, yielding *conjectures*, at the top, based on logical inferences (that might be fraught with

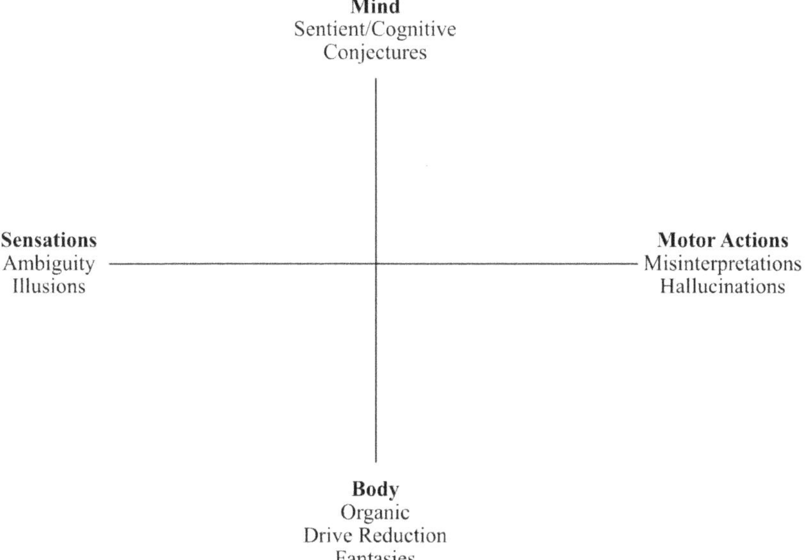

Figure 2 Contents of imagination.

risk and error) with *organic* processes, at the bottom, yielding *fantasies* and functioning in accordance with a drive reduction model of pent-up energy, followed by release or catharsis. Sentient processes can be associated with logically remote associations bringing together unexpected combinations that offer creative solutions to problems. Sometimes remote associations can be random, reflecting a breakdown in causal judgment (as in the case of psychosis). Organic processes are more closely tied to conditioning through the mediation of bodily systems. Accordingly, memories of powerful events can trigger bodily reactions tied to pleasure or pain. The contrast between remote associations and conditioning processes is fundamental here.

1.5 Acts of Imagination (Three Dimensions)

1.5.1 Overview

Discussions about "acts of imagination" can be addressed along three dimensions, encompassing; (i) time, (ii) level of consciousness or awareness, and (iii) the layered self that evolves through life (see Figure 3). The horizontal dimension of time refers to the past, present, and future, each of which pertains to different circumstances and involves distinct stimulus situations that are relevant to imagination. It bears noting the potential similarity between cognitive processes of the vertical dimension (at the top of the figure) and conscious processes referred to in this second model. The earlier model referred to contents of imaginative experience and this model

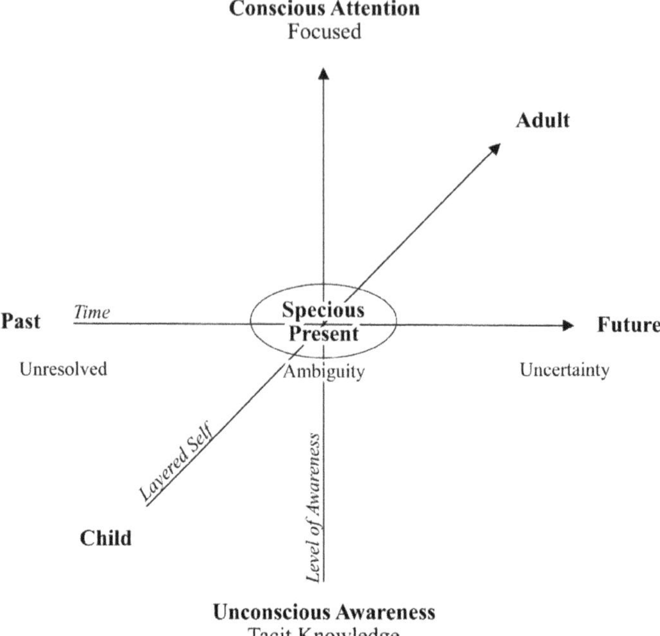

Figure 3 Acts of imagination.

addresses processes that underlie imagination. The third dimension, encompassing the layered self, is orthogonal to the 2 × 2 planes of time and consciousness. It is valuable to introduce this third dimension because people change and unfold as they grow older. Accordingly, when we move backward in time, we are not simply referring to a person's history but must take into account the stage of cognitive, personal or self-development when the event occurred. Earlier stages of childhood are experienced through different emotional and cognitive lenses (dare I use the phrase "more primitive"). While the cognitive function may be more concrete or syncretic in earlier childhood, the associated emotions are always powerful. The absence of logical constraints in childhood provides an occasion for playful dynamics that may be lost in adulthood. Recovering this dynamic is fundamental to creative happiness in adulthood.

(1) Time

The horizontal dimension of time, encompassing the present, future, and past, is fundamental to our discussion of imagination processes. Imagination gets involved under three circumstances:

(i) *Ambiguities* in the present moment.
(ii) *Uncertainties* about the future
(iii) *Unresolved* and emotionally loaded matters that linger from the past.

The "specious present" is a duration dominated by immediate perceptions of the surrounding outside world against the background of internal processes (James, 1890). It is filled with instrumental actions that may confront roadblocks and constraints requiring creative detours, as we look toward the future. An "effort after meaning" in the present also exposes a person to the potency of emotional processes. At the sensory level, *ambiguities* in sensations and appearances can lead to misperceptions and illusions that are fraught with error. At the cognitive level, ambiguity can foster false interpretations of situations with the resulting projection of our needs, hopes, and fantasies onto unsuspecting characters in life episodes. At the organic/emotional level, "suggestions meet connections," triggering or awakening long lost and perhaps even repressed emotional and embodied memories of unresolved issues in our personal lives. Thus, the specious present offers an opportunity to realize ongoing plans or address salient needs, while resolving unexpected challenges posed by external situations. It is also a doorway to salient or painful memories from the past and our hopes for the future.

Uncertainty is a primary theme regarding *future* circumstances if a crisis-like situation unexpectedly impedes the smooth flow of action. When our initial plan is *constrained*, an opportunity also arises to reframe the situation and consider alternative opportunities that might prove more efficacious ("seeing that"). This is where individual differences in life planning and the ability to adjust to blockages and engage in lateral thinking become crucial. A habit of rehearsing alternative modes of action can serve us well when we need to go around obstacles or reframe our goals. Creative planning is of the essence in the face of blockages of plans and judgment is crucial to determine whether the proposed solution is realistic. Remote associations must be tempered by pragmatic reflection.

A current event might also trigger emotionally loaded memories from the *past* regarding *unresolved* matters. Situations can spontaneously elicit emotions and expressive reactions in accordance with the principle: *suggestion meets connection*. In a sense, we digress from the immediate situation into the recesses or archeology of our minds and selves. This kind of regression can overwhelm the moment so the imagined event bears minimal similarity to the actual situation and the person's reaction may be totally unexpected. We can also experience a creative kind of regression to flexible child-like modes of play that served us well during earlier stages of our lives. Alternatively, we can become trapped in childish kinds of regression that result in emotional paralysis and inhibit productive action.

(2) Levels of Awareness

While time lies on a horizontal dimension in my model, it may be helpful to conceive of "levels of awareness or consciousness" as a vertical dimension. At the top end of the dimension, we have focused and conscious attention that reflects an effort to explicitly grasp and elucidate the meaning of a situation or event. This clarity makes it easier to consider constraints that get in the way of achieving goals and resolving needs. The bottom end of the dimension is both obscure and very interesting because this is the realm of the unconscious wherein tacit knowledge resides and it can also be a zone of purposely (suppressed) or spontaneously (repressed) hidden meanings. The unconscious will play a very important role in my story because many truths lie hidden therein and offer possibilities for personal liberation and growth.

(3) The Layered Self

The third dimension encompasses an "archeology of the self" which might sound foreboding and poetically ambiguous. In fact, it is really quite simple. I adopt the position that all layers of our personal histories, from birth through the "specious present," play an important role in shaping our imaginative activities. It is a fundamental premise in psychology that our thoughts evolve toward greater symbolic abstraction as we grow older. And yet the way we approach the world as children, in acts of play, has an element of freedom that becomes lost in the logical, conforming world of adulthood. The ability to engage in this creative and child-like "regression in service of the self" (Ignacio & Cupchik, 2020) can be contrasted with the more childish forms of behaviour that reflect frustration rather than creativity.

1.5.2 Critical Cells in Landscapes of Imagination

When we consider this three-dimensional landscape of life, two cells are of greatest interest in relation to coping and resilience versus defensive regressive activity. Emerging from the "specious present," the cell that offers the greatest potential for coping involves lucid awareness of the adult self as it turns toward planning for the future. In this context, purposeful decisions to achieve clearly defined goals can help uncover opportunities amidst uncertainty tied to the future. Strategy and planning are of the essence and embrace imaginative processes involving conscious awareness of an uncertain future related to personal needs and goals. To the extent that someone is focused on uncertainties regarding future events, strategic planning is crucial with conscious attention to details and awareness of potential outcomes. Remote associations provide a logical vehicle for bringing to bear novel and creative solutions to unexpected problems.

Perhaps the most intriguing cell reaches back to the past where fragmented and emotionally loaded syncretic residues of unresolved issues from childhood reside in the unconscious. Whereas focused light brings clarity in the first instance, darkness and failed hopes lie buried in the second. One might contrast the planful and lucid instrumental mind with metaphorical transformations that enable unresolved emotional situations to gain expression in fantasies and dreams and, in the most extreme cases, in hallucinations. The affective potency of residual memories is such that minor features of a situation in the specious present might be sufficient to automatically trigger a response that is seemingly spontaneous. The implicit or tacit potency of the reimagined event highlights the web within which it is embedded, combining or transforming sensation, emotion, and meaning in a unique way. The symbolic meaning of a situation leads to an idiosyncratic interpretation of an event that is assimilated to or experienced in the context of something that happened long ago and is, in essence, reimagined. It bears noting, of course, that fantasies of a social or erotic nature can shape future planning regarding how best to realize these goals. The role of conditioning should also be emphasized here because of the automatic and rapid way that situations awaken repressed emotional memories.

One might say that the value of psychotherapy lies in neutralizing the potency of a situation that stimulates affectively loaded recollections of the past. The web of imagination processes plays an important role here because interpreting an event or situation in the specious present brings together ambiguous perception, idiosyncratic interpretation, with affectively loaded memories to create a potentially negative experience. An appreciation of the underlying dynamics in an unresolved situation, that comes from conscious discussion with a trained therapist, can help liberate a person from the automatic re-experiencing of negative feelings tied to fear and anger. Active and conscious attention toward episodic memories, associated with pain, diminishes their potent and adverse influence on life. In essence, an important goal is to move from one cell to the other; from restrained darkness to lucid and hopeful light.

1.6 Phases of Imagination: Content and Form

Imagination involves a *web of processes* encompassing sensation, meaning, memory, emotion, and bodily states along with meaningful situations in a unified experience. Imagination also appears in different *phases* that shape the *contents* and *acts* or *forms* of experiences in different situations. The contents of imagination comprise a diverse array of representations including illusions in the present (tied to perception, images, and imagery), conjectures and imaginary associations (tied to cognition), and fantasies, dreams, and daydreams (tied to affect and

Table 1 Variations in imagination processes across time.

Time	Past Present Future
Stimulus situation	Unresolved residue Ambiguity Uncertainty
Bodily activity	Affection Sensation Cognition
Mental activity	Fantasy Illusion/delusion Hallucination

emotion). These contents can be concrete (as in an imagined future dwelling) or more symbolic (as in an archetypal image of a deity) and abstract (in the sense of a conjectured model of particles and waves or bodies and dynamic principles applied to the universe).

Form is important because it is here that imagination departs from "reality" by way of distortion or transformation. In everyday pragmatic perception, the goal is to identify the content of a situation as quickly as possible so as to implement an appropriate action and ensure survival. Time, space, sensation, and causality must all be logically present, along with a correct assessment of one's relations with others who are either literally present or accessed from memory. Imaginative episodes, on the other hand, depart from the constraints of logic that define the theme of survival. I refer here to the *plasticity of time* that, in imagined events, might speed up or slow down. Similarly, space can open up or close in to shape the phenomenology of experience as it departs from the logical structure of Western thought. Our experience of causality can break down, as in cases of paranoia wherein a person assumes that they are under attack in some way. Distortions and transformations of sensation also contribute to the intensification or enhancement of experience beyond that which is experienced in daily life. A final quality of distortion, in imagined or imaginary experiences, has to do with transformations in the experience of excessive attachment or disconnection from others.

Thus, imagination involves a web of processes encompassing all aspects of sentient and emotional life that may be unrelated to everyday reality and the goal of survival (see Table 1). The content or themes of imagined or imaginary experiences depart from the mundane qualities of everyday life. And yet, we find transformations related to imagination in every corner of daily life, including perception, cognition, and emotion. The presence of ambiguity in situations opens the door for distortions in perception in the same way that qualities of a situation can trigger idiosyncratic meanings tied to the affective residues of unresolved situations. Uncertainty about the future invites a person to reframe plans to address constraints and realize opportunities.

1.7 An Imaginative Thought Experiment

Here is a link to an article in the New York Times that discusses what have generally been referred to as "unidentified flying objects" (now referred to as "Unidentified aerial phenomena"). You do not even have to read the article. I just want you to watch the video from July 23, 2020, taken by US Navy pilots tracking "unidentified" objects in the Caribbean. The speed and movement of the cluster of objects defies current aeronautical designs in the US Navy.

www.nytimes.com/2020/07/23/us/politics/pentagon-ufo-harry-reid-navy .html[2]

You do not have to believe in the veracity of the video. Just watch the video, please, which is authentic from the viewpoint of the military.

There are different ways to address these little UFOs in relation to imagination. First of all, there do not have to be living creatures on board. Like our cars today, they can be self- or remotely driven. Here is the imagination exercise. One approach to this imagination exercise is to ask you to imagine potential living creatures on board. A standard default would be to assume they look like "ET" of movie fame. I am suggesting a different approach which is to imagine that you are actually on board one of those "spaceships" and required to send back a report about the "human" organisms on Earth. That is your "science project," so to speak. Remember that you have never seen humans, or flora (plant life) and fauna (animal life).

Your assignment is to send back a report just about the humans, and you want to be a good celestial naturalist and as accurate as possible. After all, if you could get here and choose Earth among the seemingly infinite objects in space, then your science of description regarding matter and mind must be well beyond what we have on Earth at this time. I note in passing, by the way, that all the developments of earthly science have as yet to figure out how "mind" is related to "matter." You are examining these earthly creatures at a distance because we are skeptical about any reports of interactions between people from outer space and us. You want to keep things simple and are not going to address social interaction or social groups.

The value of this "imagination" exercise is that we peel back the surface of language and get down to basics. What is a minimal or parsimonious model to report about humans on Earth? The two-dimensional model introduced earlier can be very helpful. The horizontal dimension (see Figure 1) juxtaposes sensation (sensory input) on the left and action (motor output) on the right end. The vertical dimension contrasts bodily organ systems (e.g., heart, lungs, and so forth) at the bottom with brain activity (related to sentience) at the top. The bodily organs are

[2] Blumenthal, R., & Kean, L. (2021). *No Longer in Shadows, Pentagon's U.F.O. Unit Will Make Some Findings Public*. www.nytimes.com/2020/07/23/us/politics/pentagon-ufo-harry-reid-navy.html.

tied to affects and emotions, whereas brain activity is layered, monitoring the body while being the repository of life's development across species. Consciousness, as such, embraces these bodily functions in the context of a social world and all that implies by way of rules and their impact on individuals.

What exactly will you report back to the mother ship? Will you simply describe the structure of the living organism? Will you address the diversity of language (i.e., sounds) and how it manifests in different ways around the globe? How much is enough? Will it reflect fact or simply conjecture based on limited data? Even visitors from outer space face the challenge of accuracy; stability is an illusion even for them. One last point; while all these nuances can be described, one thing eludes us – consciousness itself. By the way, an artist friend is a serious consumer of sci-fi programming but rejects totally the idea that there are other conscious "beings" in the universe. Go figure!

1.8 Summary

I have proposed that imagination touches everyday life in a profound way and will elaborate still more in later sections. It incorporates sensations, thoughts, and feelings within a unified experience that is relatively free from the constraints of an immediate moment yet situated in a physical and social world. Therein lies the "web of imagination." Two central themes underlying imagination encompass challenges to personal or collective survival (in both the animal and human worlds) and an "effort after meaning" to more deeply understand a situation that is distinctive to human sentient life. On the dimension of time, imagination plays an instrumental role when our plans run into roadblocks, and we need to strategize regarding how best to deal with the uncertainties of the future. Ambiguities in a situation can also produce sensory-based illusions or social misinterpretations, opening the door for the projection of fanciful interpretations to address the meaning of an event. Events in the present can trigger unresolved memories or long-buried traumas from our past.

The role of consciousness has to be considered here in contrasting ways. Conscious, reflective awareness enables us to take stock of situations and logically consider alternative strategies for realizing goals or handling frustrations. But it is in the unconscious where powerful episodic memories are buried only to find release in dreams and fantasies or even hallucinations. All this takes place against the background of human development and the gradual unfolding of detached and rational analysis in relation to family and culture. Accordingly, the most interesting cells of the 2 (time) × 2 (consciousness) × 2 (development) model involve (1) conscious lucid planning for the future based on logical inference and (2) unconscious emotional experiences linked to the remote past of childhood when we were passive participants in events.

We can also be tuned to ways that imagination shapes experiences in our lives because the content has a metaphorical quality and is framed by distortions in time (faster or slower), space (opening or closing), sensation (heightened or flattened), causality (less logical and more arbitrary), and problems in social connections (increased isolation). In short, we always need to ask ourselves an important question: Is my understanding of a situation accurate or somehow distorted by unresolved needs and desires? In the end, engaging in "acts of noticing" tunes us to the texture and meaning of critical situations that offer both constraints and opportunities. Being aware of how our mind operates to foster clarity or project distortion is a pathway to mental health. This applies to all domains in which instrumental reasoning has to accommodate fantasied changes.

Consider the case of cosmetic surgery in which a patient has to decide how much change to an area of their face or body is sufficient to please them (Lindner & Cupchik, 2024). We have emphasized the importance of cultivating a holistic attitude toward potential bodily changes. This attitude is established when patients are empowered to transform how they will look from baseline (their current state) to an ideal final result. Developments in AI and technology provide an avenue for putting imagined change literally in the hands of the patient. Change is therefore seen in the context of the whole original face or body. This process falls within the classic tradition of the Just Noticeable Difference and Weber's Law (see Boring, 1950) regarding noticing differences in the degree of change in a stimulus (in this case, a feature of the human body). The underlying principle of "less is more" applies here in the sense that less change will appear sufficient when a patient sees transformation in relation to the original baseline. By encouraging a subjective sense of self, the "locus of control" (Rotter, 1966) and a sense of "self-efficacy" is preserved within the patient. Doing so makes them less reliant on the seemingly "objective" and detached opinions of others. Fostering a proper balance of "instrumental" and "expressive" change in how people see themselves provides a valuable direction for cosmetic surgery practice.

The UFO experiment provided an opportunity to engage in parsimonious reflection about the minimal amount of information that would provide an alien world with some sense of how human organisms are related to and yet different from flora and fauna. This is grounded in bodily systems related to sensation, action, organic systems, and sentient systems that preserve an embedded hierarchy of life on Earth among living human organisms. Language, a sentient quality, provides an avenue for reflection about ourselves and our worlds in a social context. This encompasses the role of conversation in human life whereby we communicate, both with ourselves and others, that which we take for granted as real. It extends to moments of ambiguity, illusion, and uncertainty wherein we can turn to others for help or admit to ourselves that we are unsure about boundaries both within ourselves and between ourselves and surrounding physical, organic, and social worlds.

2 The Arc of Imagination in Aesthetic Experience

2.1 Aesthetic versus Everyday Imagination

In Section 1, we considered how imagination plays an important role in everyday life and discovered that it is lurking in the shadow of every experience and at the heart of how we construe our realities. Accordingly, what is *not* imagination, and can it be observed? Ambiguity in the moment, uncertainty about the future, and unresolved residues from the past are all relevant. Ambiguity provides an opportunity to project needs and concerns into a situation. Uncertainty opens the door for creative problem-solving in the light of unexpected opportunities, sometimes in the midst of a crisis. Situations can also trigger long-buried emotional memories of unresolved events from the past that unexpectedly reappear in the moment. Does imagination play a role in aesthetic experience differing from that in everyday life? There are two parts to this answer. First, aesthetic episodes, and related experiences, differ in fundamental ways from everyday experiences. Second, aesthetic works that stimulate experiences are structured differently from everyday events and, hence, processed differently.

According to the pragmatic attitude of everyday life, our goal is to identify people, animals, or objects that are relevant to survival and adaptation, as rapidly as possible. The sensory information out of which these images emerge is discarded on route to object identification. This *cognitive bias* is prevalent in everyday life so it can be a challenge to deautomatize perception and turn away from the habit of rushing to identify the contents of experiences. A central challenge of art education is to slow down this pragmatic habit so students can attend to and identify the organized sensory qualities that constitute what we call "style." Authors, artists, singers, and dancers experience and preserve the sounds, conversations, shapes, colours, textures, and movements of their worlds as raw materials of the creative process, saving them without prejudice in an aesthetic vault of episodic memories. There is no "bias" here; rather, a rich resource of sounds, shapes, and movements to be retrieved later for works as yet unknown.

To recreate these acts of noticing and creativity, and to grasp the challenge, imagine being in a rowboat observing an island at sunset on a windy day. Can you see the little waves with sunlight reflecting off them? Now imagine recreating that scene in a painting. You need to capture the setting sun, the island, and clouds (and sky) reflecting off the surface of the water, so you apply dabs of paint to the surface of the canvas. Since we are so used to seeing photographs of sunsets, all these little dabs of paint can be quite distracting. As beholders, we must learn to balance the subject matter of our little painting; the sunset, water, and island, while noticing or appreciating how the dabs of colour are organized to shape our experiences. This is an Impressionist "act of noticing" and related creative ("tachiste") gestures.

How then is aesthetic imagination different from imagination in everyday life, given that illusions, dreams, daydreams, and even hallucinations happen spontaneously in everyday life? We can begin by distinguishing imaginative creation and imaginative reception. Consider the creative artist or author flowing through the "stream of consciousness" of everyday life. From a pragmatic perspective, we move through life completing tasks. But the artist or author, in contrast, engages in "acts of noticing" shapes, textures, and colours or hearing sounds and conversations that become the raw materials of creativity. The act of creation is, in fact, an act of imagination because these raw materials are selected and transported to canvases of the mind where they are sorted and organized within frames that are called paintings or stories. The process of selection transforms these different elements into coherent and unified images or narratives in accordance with the aesthetic principle of "unity amidst diversity." The sensory richness of daily life becomes the material foundation of creative actions that yield intense and rich works.

Aesthetic receptive imagination, on the other hand, happens during culturally mandated episodes or events and in formal places, or even when we are alone. When we visit museums or attend plays or dance performances, we enter into a special space and an experience of time. Whereas ambiguity in everyday situations is forced upon a person, the "willing suspension of disbelief" reflects an intentional decision (an "attitude") to observe and experience something in a special way. Ironically, ambiguity plays a role both in everyday life and in aesthetic experiences. Ambiguity challenges interpretation in everyday life but invites projection and connection in aesthetic experiences, telling us something about life. When survival is the dominant theme, errors of interpretation come with a price. In contrast, when aesthetic diversion is the main goal, ambiguity is a gift, inviting us to be playful. These experiences have intrinsic rather than extrinsic or instrumental and goal-oriented value (Berlyne, 1971). This shift away from the practical realities of everyday life can happen even as we observe a beautiful sunset or light shimmering on waves in a lake. My focus here is on aesthetic experiences associated with cultural artifacts and events, such as going to a museum or musical performance, attending a play or ballet, and so forth. But it can be equally applied to experiences in nature.

In essence, we have a kind of dance between those who create and those who receive. Aesthetic works reflect the results of a creative act of selection, organization, and representation in images, sounds, tastes, and so forth. Formally speaking, paintings or stories combine subject matter (or content) and style (or form) in a unique way. The image of a layer cake is helpful here.

The basic layer comprises the medium (such as oil paint or watercolour in paintings) that is organized by the artist in a unique way during the process of application (by brush, palette knife, or whatever). The themes of "surface" and "depth" in media research (Cupchik, 2011) can be linked to the horizontal (sensory-motor) and vertical (mind-body) dimensions of the Content Model in Figure 2 respectively. The sensory-motor dimension is related to a desire to modulate feelings of pleasure and arousal when selecting among media offerings (Principle of *affective covariation*). Accordingly, a nostalgic mood might lead a person to watch a romantic movie that produces pleasurable and warm feelings. Action films might be more appropriate for someone who is bored and needs a vicarious energizing experience. Indeed, authors and film makers can intentionally seek to modulate these feelings of pleasure and excitement. This kind of "reactive model" involves a homeostatic process because selection of an appropriate stimulus will resolve the need and eventually terminate the experience (Cupchik, 1995). This does not require deeper processing to determine the value of a stimulus and related response and, hence, is more superficial.

A more "reflective model" is associated with the principle of "emotional elaboration" wherein the spectator or reader interprets situations described in a work and explores underlying layers of meaning in relation to lived experiences. Personal absorption is reflected in this "effort after meaning" and involves a combination of imagination, emotion, and thought. This ensures a greater depth of understanding, in contrast to the appraisal-based judgments guiding "affective covariation" judgments. Searching for coherence in an unfolding narrative (a play, novel, or film) provides an opportunity to critically embrace the episode and can lead to a fresh perspective on life. This interpretive effort provides a basis for long-term attachment to works that are challenging and personally meaningful. The value of "emotional elaboration" has been shown in studies dealing with the reception of short stories (Cupchik & Laszlo, 1994), novels (Braun & Cupchik, 2001), sculptures (Cupchik & Shereck, 1998), and paintings (Cupchik & Gignac, 2007). The medium encompasses those elements that are observed and aesthetically digested by creative people as they move through life. The organization of these basic elements is an important feature of what is called "style." Training is required to attend to this layer and appreciate its defining qualities through a process of "deautomatization" because, in everyday pragmatic perception, it is not attended to as we rush to object identification. The content or subject matter of an artwork emerges, so to speak, from the careful organization of stylistic elements through acts of representation. There is always a story behind the content, and it may require training to appreciate the full narrative (i.e., iconography) underlying what is depicted (e.g., in a religious painting, for example) and to go beyond the work into the culture from which it emerged (i.e., iconology). Successful communication between creative people and beholders, readers, or audience members takes place when the content of a work awakens the imagination of the recipient because of shared meanings, feelings, and emotions. This is a clear case of *suggestion meets connection* between creator and recipient and is also related to the "web of imagination" combining sensation, cognition, and memory within holistic experiences.

There is an interesting tradeoff here. In highly representational (i.e., realistic) artworks, there are rules about how space is represented (i.e., affordances), so the emerging artwork looks like or simulates the natural world in accordance with the *principle of mimesis* (i.e., imitation). The sensory organization of the work, in essence, recreates everyday experience and we read the framed image "as if" it was a representation of everyday life. In more abstract works, realism or accuracy (*mimesis*) does not determine the organization of these stylistic elements (i.e., shapes or colours) and it is, therefore, more challenging to "read" or interpret a work that expresses unique ideas and feelings of the artists or their community. The more salient and unique the stylistic qualities, the harder it is to identify the subject matter. This absence of clarity opens the door for imaginatively projecting meaning onto ambiguous images. Accordingly, *ambiguity fosters projection.*

How does the subject matter of an artwork stimulate the imagination? The content of an artwork, literary or theatrical piece, or a dance performance has symbolic value. If one is familiar with the culture or genre, it is easier to "decode" or identify the meaning of the content and scene as a whole. Accordingly, the content requires a cultural dictionary with which to interpret the symbolic meaning of various elements in a scene. However, this challenge offers a kind of ambiguity onto which the viewer might project meaning in accordance with the principle, *suggestion meets connection*. Beholders interpret the ambiguity of an image, assimilating it to what they know or in relation to questions they might have. In this way, imagination enables them to project personal meaning onto the ambiguity of an artwork, a story, a dance, and so on.

The situation becomes more interesting as the image departs from *mimesis* or verisimilitude, in other words, a direct replication or simulation of everyday life. It is one thing to misidentify or reinterpret the meaning of a symbolic element in an artwork of story and quite another thing to be distracted by form that is salient. This salience might occur because objects are arbitrarily coloured and, hence, unfamiliar or ambiguous (e.g., a green fire truck). However, distortions in space (that opens up or closes in and departs from that which governs everyday life), time (that speeds up or slows down), sensory qualities (colours or textures that are unfamiliar), causality (that defies causal logic), or social connection (defies the logic of social interaction) open the door of the imagination onto which recreations are projected. Departure from the familiar structure of everyday life provides a context for imaginative interpretation, reinterpretation, or misinterpretation; *ambiguity fosters projection.*

The arc of imagination, during aesthetic episodes, is tied to the depth of appreciation and a comparison between Popular Art, Avant Garde Art, and High Art is relevant here. At the surface level of popular culture, individuals and audiences can respond to familiar and easily identifiable subject matter in a scene. This familiarity produces superficial feelings that accompany experiences. Avant Garde Art belongs to "insider groups" who have learned the secrets of how to interpret or decode unfamiliar subject matters and scripts associated with scenarios or scenes. It is fundamentally cerebral. High Art has two sides. On the one hand, it refers to works in museum settings requiring knowledge about subject matter and style that presumes specialized training. On the other hand, High Art can touch upon deeper emotions that are awakened by scenes depicting events possessing historical, cultural, or personal meaning. These works can stimulate the imagination to digress into one's own personal and cultural life.

Thus, the arc of imagination begins with the knowledge that "this is not everyday life" and unfolds in accordance with relations between subject matter and style. At a surface level, viewers and audience members can enter a fantasy depicting familiar themes and meanings which may be accompanied by pleasure or excitement. The deeper the aesthetic experience, the more complex the imaginative process so that aesthetic works take us further away from everyday life and permit us to project meanings and feelings. This is the world of mythical creatures and stories. It is here that catharsis can occur because the symbolic and camouflaged nature of the aesthetic work permits hidden and conflicting emotions to be released. In the midst of ambiguity, imagination finds a place to be engaged so that the web of life is released in perceptions, meanings, bodily reactions, and emotions. The aesthetic situation or event provides a context in which these deeper emotions can be legitimately experienced and expressed.

2.2 The "Thinking-Eye" and the "Being-I"

A contrast between the "Thinking-eye" and the "Being-I" is relevant here (Cupchik, 1999). The "Thinking-eye" of the artist is planful so that the work unfolds in a logical way in accordance with the principles of design. The skilled eye of a recipient can decode or interpret the image, scene, or story within the constraints of culture. The "Being-I" is more personal so that an emerging work of art embodies meaning from the life of the artist or a story conveys episodic memories from the author's life that are transformed to protect the innocent. The principle of "suggestion meets connection" refers to a more personal bridge that is built between the work and the individual whose emotional memories are awakened. The "Thinking-eye" is generally tied to knowledge and choice, whereas the "Being-I" spontaneously explores an artwork in search of personal meaning tied to deeper emotions.

While artists are engaged in the "Thinking-eye," planning and logically executing their artworks, the "Being-I" of personal life might unconsciously shape both the choice of subject matter and aspects of style. Without consciously thinking about it, the artist might choose to embed an element in the work that is rich in personal symbolic meaning. The same might be said regarding stylistic decisions. To the extent that the style of a painting is soft-edge, with ambiguous boundaries between people and objects, there is room to project images and meanings onto the ambiguous spaces. Artists are continually shifting between (objective) "doing," applying painting in a structured way, and (subjective) "undergoing," experiencing the emerging image. It is here, during the process of creation, that unconscious materials might "leak in" to shape the work. There is a trade-off such that, if the artist is logically concentrated on the subject matter, emotionalized imagination can sneak inadvertently into the act of painting through the way a brush is held or paint is applied. Conversely, the artist might be committed to a particular stylistic act, but unconscious meaning might populate the work with symbolically rich content. This is the beauty of art that comprises a layering of sensory and symbolic content. Artists can focus on one structured sensation or selective content, while leaving the door open for imagination to sneak in and shape the unmonitored channel. This raises the question as to whether great geniuses of the Renaissance were subject to this kind of "leakage" dynamic, or did they consciously monitor all facets of their arc of creation?

The juxtaposition between the "Thinking-eye" and the "Being-I" is most salient in acts of creation and acts of reception. The painter, poet, or playwright experiences both in the act of "doing," being deeply involved in the process of creation and, yet, standing back to "objectively" see how the work is progressing. Generally speaking, viewers, readers, and audiences are simply "undergoing" the work. But they may have different levels of knowledge enabling them to simulate or adopt the artist's or author's creative viewpoint and imagine how the work progressed over time. The act of "undergoing" ranges from identifying surface layers of information about subject matter elements and formally identifying the style via the "Thinking-eye" to deeper levels of resonance where ambiguity in the symbolic meaning of a work, and how it is executed, turns the viewer into a hidden artist whose experience touches the deepest layers of the Being-I.

2.2.1 Aesthetic Distance

This discussion of the arc of imagination brings us to the topic of "aesthetic distance" and concerns the relationship between the viewer or audience member and a creative work. What is the optimal distance that a viewer, reader, or audience member should adopt in relation to engagement with creative works? This is a challenging question because a main point behind aesthetics is that we know the work is not "real" and choose to enter an experience that requires imagination and from which we can learn about ourselves. Edward Bullough (1880–1934) addressed this paradoxical quality to the aesthetic state "in which *we know* a thing *not* to exist, but *accept its existence*" (Bullough, 1912, p. 113). According to his *principle of concordance*, our goal should involve optimal involvement without excessive self-absorption; "*utmost decrease of Distance without its disappearance*" (Bullough, 1912, p. 94). This principle reflects the need for a balance between realism, which helps us appreciate a scene (the "Thinking-eye"), and personal resonance (the "Being-I"), which draws us in emotionally.

What does this discussion of "aesthetic distance" have to do with the arc of imagination? We enter aesthetic episodes, knowing they are not, in fact, "real" and do so both with the anticipation of pleasure and as an opportunity to reflect on the meaning embedded in the works. In a sense, we recreate the event in our minds, shaping it with knowledge of the genre and lending it nuance because of personal meanings that are awakened. Aesthetic episodes occur outside the pragmatic flow of everyday life and its theme of survival. They take place in the interstices, the space between fantasy and reality. It is the gift of artists and authors to optimize this distance, offering dramatic and humanly interesting situations in the problems being posed. Accordingly, we are exposed to situations that can trigger unresolved emotional residues and have an opportunity to experience the release of pent-up emotions, while at the same time reflecting on the situations (i.e., our problems). Aesthetic imagination offers a pathway to the transcendence of personal dilemmas and to achieving emotional equanimity as we look into an uncertain future.

Aesthetic episodes, in which we expose ourselves to the creative works of others, can also lead to the recreation of trauma. In the case of "*under-distancing*," the subject matter can be "'crudely naturalistic,' 'harrowing,' 'repulsive in its realism'" (Bullough, 1912, p. 94) which, at the time Bullough was writing in the early twentieth century, could pertain to repressed sexual themes. Accordingly, the more mundane the reference, the higher the probability that the episode might recreate the experience of everyday lived experiences, in which case the person is overcome with negative emotion. A case of "*over-distancing*" occurs when the work "produces the impression of improbability, artificiality, emptiness or absurdity" (Bullough, 1912, p. 94) and the aesthetic moment is lost because the imagination, while working overtime, cannot treat the event as if it were real. One might say that a goal of aesthetic experience is to modulate the arc of imagination so the work is appreciated at an optimal distance. In a proper combination of imagination and distance, "real tragedy ... truly appreciated, is not sad ... it is the homage to the great and exceptional in the man who in a last effort of spiritual tension can rise to confront blind, crowning Necessity even in his crushing defeat" (Bullough, 1912, p. 104). In other words, we recreate the event in our mind's eye in such a way as not to be overcome with emotionalized recollections but to reflect upon it and achieve an element of wisdom.

The British psychoanalyst Donald Winnicott (1896–1971) explored the compensatory function that *imaginative play activity* can have for temporarily fulfilling an emotional need. He described the value of investing emotion in "transitional objects" to which a person is deeply attached (think of the favourite stuffed animal of your childhood). From his perspective, the "true self" is expressed in these spontaneous and authentic experiences (Winnicott, 1965). There is a delicate analogy here between childhood experiences of separation from the mother and the roots of Bullough's "psychical distance." For Winnicott, the child is challenged to become separate from the mother and "transitional objects," such as stuffed animals to which one is emotionally attached, can ease the process of individuation (Winnicott, 1971). Accordingly, "The place where cultural experience is located is in the *potential space* between the individual and the environment (originally the object)" (Winnicott, 1971, p. 100). Emotionalized imagination and attachment find a meaningful place in this paradoxical aesthetic space between the "*subjective object*" and the "*object objectively perceived.*"

Accordingly, Bullough's optimal "psychical distance" and Winnicott's "transitional space" serve the same purpose of creating an imaginal safe space for the development of the individual and autonomous self. One might even suggest that the child's adapting to distance from a caring parent establishes the paradigm for optimal aesthetic engagement, based on imagination, thereby accommodating emotional needs and an "effort after meaning." Accordingly, "The 'true self' can feel strong attachment to an image with which it identifies even though the reasons may not be explicitly clear because the image serves as a metaphor for the person's life" (Winnicott, 1965, in Cupchik, 2016, p. 189). Exploring this metaphor lies at the heart of successful therapy wherein hidden emotionally loaded meanings gain expression and long-lost issues can be explored, thereby liberating the person from unresolved residues of life. This represents a process whereby imagination provides an avenue for exploring unconscious meanings.

Imagination plays an important role in this lifelong process of individuation, the development of a separate sense of self, and early experiences establish the conditions for imaginal activity. It is perhaps for this reason that we associate imagination with childhood and the idea that it is progressively abandoned as we move into the pragmatic realism of adulthood. Recall the premise of my work which is centred on the web image whereby bodily/organic emotion, sensation, and thought are unified within a framework called imagination. Imagination takes place in the specious present wherein "suggestion meets connection," extending into the uncertainty of future events through conjecture, and to emotionally loaded residues of the past that may be long buried. Acts of imagination serve as a glue, enabling these tacit experiences, where emotion is dissociated from content and context, to gain symbolic expression. Reflecting on these products of imagination lies at the heart of therapeutic and aesthetic experiences.

It is for this reason that acts of imagination, and related experiences, have a holistic quality that is central to Gestalt psychology. The transformations in how children experience their worlds provide a foundation for acts of imagination. Heinz Werner carefully described this transformation "from a state of relative globality and undifferentiatedness towards states of increasing differentiation and hierarchical integration" (Werner & Kaplan, 1963, p. 7). Globality is associated with experiences that spontaneously combine sensory, affective, and motor aspects into a unified whole, in a personal and unique way (Werner, 1978). Expressive (i.e., physiognomic) qualities are experienced before sensory information is identified which is what happens in aesthetic experiences (Arnheim, 1971). Cognitive and social development are defined by more abstract and symbolic thinking. Self-world differentiation is related to a greater ability to appreciate the "geometric-technical" qualities of images and useful tools. Even as we grow older, we preserve our sensory and emotional attachments to situations and life episodes that are personally meaningful. It is these situations to which we imaginatively and spontaneously respond in stories and plays.

The arc of imagination in aesthetic episodes closely parallels perceptual, emotional, and cognitive development. First, we experience the sensory qualities of an artwork in a global, holistic, and orderly way within a glance of just 50 *ms* (Cupchik & Berlyne, 1979). It is in this earliest stage of experience that the presence or absence of defining edges separate objects in artworks (Mureika, Dyer, & Cupchik, 2005). This contrast between hard and soft edges, also referred to as *linear-versus-painterly* (Wölfflin, 1915/1950), is fundamental to art history. The relative orderliness of this first stage or layer of perception provides a background or context from which the subject matter emerges in our experiences. Order provides a sense of calm and disorder creates an experience of tension. Second, the content or subject matter of a work can elicit reflection about the theme of the painting or trigger emotionally loaded memories that either draw us in or repel us because negative emotions are triggered. This is how our experience emerges and is constructed over time in the arc of imagination. Feelings that are by-products of the earliest stage of perception colour subsequent thoughts and the experience of a work according to the principle of "feeling before knowing." As a work is processed more deeply over time, relevant themes are uncovered and this kind of "emotional elaboration" is the foundation for strong attachment to personally meaningful aesthetic works.

This holistic process is elegantly described in John Dewey's (1934) book, *Art as Experience*. He addressed "situations and episodes" wherein "every successive part flows freely, without seam and without unfilled blanks, into what ensues" (Dewey, 1934, p. 36). Accordingly, aesthetic experience "has pattern and structure, because it is not just doing and undergoing in alternation, but consists of them in relationship" (Dewey, 1934, p. 44). As the aesthetic episode "moves toward a close" (Dewey, 1934, p. 41), it also has a "quality that rounds out an experience into completeness and unity as emotional" (p. 41). Artists possess imaginative flexibility, *reacting* to powerful situations ("undergoing") that elicit emotional memories while engaging in *action* ("doing") to realize goals while painting. Artists are able to focus internally on their experiences and then shift to an external viewpoint to critically evaluate the progress of their work.

This shifting between holistic and analytical attention has very interesting implications. The artist's imaginative flexibility fosters a regression "in service of the ego" (Kris, 1952) and of the "self" (Ignacio & Cupchik, 2020) which can access material from unconscious experiences ("seeing as") and integrate it within an emerging composition ("seeing that"). While artists and authors create in the "specious present," they can spontaneously and unconsciously access unresolved emotional memories as potential material. A trade-off dynamic can be at play here that provides an avenue for emotionalized imagination through a process we referred to earlier as "emotional leakage" (Cupchik, 2016). If attention is paid to the subject matter, emotion can unexpectedly leak into how the work is actually executed. While the artist might be focused on copying the model accurately, the tension in the brushstroke might reflect an awakened emotion theme to which the artist is not tuned. Conversely, if attention is paid to how the work is executed and its style, the choice of subject matter may not be carefully controlled.

Unconscious dynamics can shape either the choice of subject matter or expressive aspects of style without the artist or author being in any way aware that this is happening. There is a downside to exploring the psychological foundations behind an artist's attachment to his or her own work. Once the motive is revealed and understood, the theme no longer needs to be explored and so that part of the artist's repertoire shuts down. Making an artist self-conscious about the spontaneous expression of emotion in the choice of emotionally symbolic thematic elements, or the expressive power of a stylistic decision, eliminates the spontaneous aspects of imaginative creativity. Regressive processes are best left in the closet of imagination.

In summary, artists and authors embody and embed meaning in their unfolding works, even as they shift between subjectively engaged and objectively detached perspectives. If attention is focused on stylistic matters, the choice of subject matter is not considered in a reflective manner. Conversely, if attention is focused on the subject matter, attention may not be directed to some nuances of form or style. In realistic painting, the function of style is to create a logical setting within which to populate the narrative. In more impressionist or expressionist styles of painting, the feeling of the form can take precedence over that which is rendered in the narrative. The creative process opens a door for unresolved and emotionally loaded matters to find their way into the subject or style or a work without the person's awareness. This raises an interesting issue as to whether the "great geniuses" of the Renaissance were free from regressive dynamics.

The central point here is that aesthetic works can stimulate imagination at each phase of the creation and reception process because *stability is an illusion*. In other words, our perception of the world unfolds over time and aesthetic materials and episodes are important because the orderly or disorderly nature of sensation (that lies at the heart of aesthetic creation and reception) provides a context or framework within which the emerging subject matter or narrative unfolds. Ambiguity in the sensory structure stimulates our feelings of illusion and interacts with ambiguity in the meaning of the subject matter. This provides a screen, so to speak, onto which we can project meanings, feelings, and unresolved needs and also construe possibilities that others may have overlooked. Culture provides a frame in which this process unfolds.

2.3 Cultural Dynamics of Aesthetic Imagination

In the West, there are contrasting viewpoints as to how imagination shapes aesthetic experience. There is a long history in the West contrasting two kinds of processes, one dealing with form and the other with embodied expression. The

Greek Apollonian tradition stressed formal discipline while Dionysian tradition favored sensual emotionality. It was repeated in the Italian Renaissance contrast between a Florentine emphasis on *desegno* in comparison with the expressive *colore* tradition of Venice, as well as in the later contrast between British Enlightenment theory versus German Romanticism, or a contrast in nineteenth-century German aesthetic theory between *formalism* and *projectionism*. The fundamental opposition is between reason and society in British Enlightenment thought and the irrationalism of individuals as embodied in German Romanticism (Ellenberger, 1970). The Enlightenment favoured voluntary social contracts emphasizing reason that shaped human progress, whereas Romanticism was oriented toward our intimate relationship with nature in relation to the depths of the "soul" and emotional life.

2.3.1 Enlightenment Aesthetics

The British Enlightenment and French Neoclassical logical principles of aesthetics in the mid eighteenth century maintained that powerful dramatic illusion was created by the unity of time, place, and action controlling audience responses through a process of *mimesis* (Burwick, 1991). This brings to mind the opening scenes of 007 films in which audiences are caught up in the rapidly unfolding action that is tied to one simple theme: survival. There is little room for reflection or transcendence in this approach to theatre. In a similar way, the German Formalist approach to art of the early nineteenth century downplayed anything symbolic or meaningful in favour of relations among properties of lines, planes, colours, and tones that shaped viewer experiences. In this "science of form," there was no room for ideas about "ethical, emotional, intellectual, and sentimental 'intrusions' into the act of aesthetic perception" that might be embodied in "content" (Mallgrave & Ikonomou, 1994, p. 10). The focus should be on formal structure without distraction by emotional content or "waking dreaminess" (Mallgrave & Ikonomou, 1994), both in theatre and while listening to music. Simply put, the stimulus controls the reactions of audiences or viewers who are simply along for the ride, as action unfolds, real or implied.

2.3.2 German Romanticism

German Romanticism, in the tradition of Goethe and Schiller, was focused on metamorphoses underlying the emotional and intellectual development of individuals (and even plants, for Goethe). As a consequence, the dynamic interplay of forces in the conscious and unconscious mind would shape aesthetic experiences. It should not be surprising that German philosophers would focus on lived experiences that result from the interpretation of social episodes. In an aesthetic context, August Schlegel (1767–1845) grounded "aesthetic illusion in imagination" (Burwick, 1991, p. 193) so that we treat theatre "as a 'waking dream, to which we voluntarily surrender ourselves'" (p. 194). These illusions are shaped by events on the theatrical stage so that reality and illusion actually coexist. "The reality of the dramatic dialogue is that the text is written; the illusion is that dramatic dialogue is spoken spontaneously" (Burwick, 1991, p. 201). Audience members understand that dialogue only appears spontaneous, and this sustains the illusion. In other words, audiences actively participate in treating events on the stage "as if" they were real. Schlegel was responsible for translating Shakespeare into German, providing meaningful social situations into which audiences could project themselves. The boundaries between audience members and the stage disappear into the web of imagination. Winnicott would approve of this transitional dramatic space.

A similar treatment of artistic experience was central to a Romantic theory of artistic expression in the middle of nineteenth-century Germany. The main idea was that symbolic content in artwork triggers empathic responses in viewers. Robert Vischer (1847–1933) theorized about "projection" whereby the content of artworks stimulated or conditioned sensory and emotional processes in an automatic way. The highest level "engages the ... imaginative activity of the mind" (Mallgrave & Ikonomou, 1994, p. 22) so that images of the sensory event are combined with images of the "self" and viewers *project* their feelings onto the object as part of "a harmonious emotive process" (p. 27). Theodor Lipps (1903/1962) carried this idea into the twentieth century, arguing that our bodily (kinesthetic) sensations, and associated emotional experiences, mirror (are synchronized with) the expressive qualities of persons or objects. The resulting emotional experience is attributed to or projected onto the evocative stimulus through a process of "feeling into" or *Einfühlung* (a concept developed by Vischer). Baldwin (1930) similarly highlighted the importance of "aesthetic immediacy" and *affective revival* so that the artist, and to some degree the observer, "*lives in or finds himself involved with* the work of art" identifying "their own inner movement of feeling with that of the work of art" (p. 19).

In accordance with the (projectionist) approach of Gestalt Psychology, Rudolf Arnheim (1904–2007) took strong exception to the Formalist belief of Fechner that "the ultimate truth resided in direct sensory experience" (Arnheim, 1985, p. 859) and a striving for pleasure rather than a search for meaning related to the self that "led to the insipid and unfruitful aesthetic conception of art as a source of pleasure" (Arnheim, 1985, p. 861). Arnheim (1954/1971) maintained that people discern expressive qualities of artworks directly without being explicitly aware of the specific underlying structural features. Indeed, the "priority of physiognomic properties should not come as a surprise" (Arnheim, 1971, p. 430) because "expression is a configuration of forces" (Arnheim, 1971, p. 434) and "an inherent characteristic of perceptual patterns" (Arnheim, 1971, p. 433). This is the foundation of the principle of "feeling before knowing."

Accordingly, the subject matter of an artwork is spontaneously experienced in relation to its expressive qualities. "In the great works of art, the deepest significance is transmitted to the eye with powerful directness by the perceptual characteristics of the compositional pattern" (Arnheim, 1954, p. 436). As a consequence, a mere configuration of forces in the artwork transfers to the mental world where "Motifs like rising and falling, dominance and submission, weakness and strength, harmony and discord, struggle and conformance, underlie all existence" (Arnheim, 1971, p. 434). This describes a metaphorical process whereby viewers find "the symbolic meaning expressed in concrete happening, the sensing of the universal in the particular" (Arnheim, 1971, p. 436). The meaning attributed to a painting therefore reflects a figure/ground relationship in which its subject matter resonates with the expressive qualities embedded in its style. It is this emphasis upon the spontaneous expressive quality of artworks, and the interrelationship among levels, that distinguishes the dynamic Gestalt approach from Formalism and the more linear information theory that emerged from it.

2.3.3 Chinese Landscape Painting

While the aesthetic foundations of Western thought are founded on a model of perception that sends or passes along sensory information to imagination and the knowing mind, Ancient Chinese aesthetics adopts a very different approach and understanding (Law, 2011). Simply put, the Chinese tradition of landscape painting, better known as *shanshui*, makes literal reference to mountains (*shan*) and waters (*shui*) as far back as the fourth century AD in Daoist philosophy. The difference is best illustrated in the story of the monk Zong Bing who visited many mountains and rivers throughout his life in search of enlightenment from nature. In his later years, an illness made it impossible for him to seek wisdom through contemplation of the natural world. He decided to use his paintbrush to depict the mountains and rivers he had visited and meditated in front of the finished image on his wall as a kind of *woyou* (spiritual mind travelling in bed). These images reflected an accumulation of episodes of being in nature and his treatise on painting reflected his changing perspective as his mind travelled from one point to the next. The absence of a fixed perspective on Chinese landscape painting "incites the audience's vision to roam and wander around the image, and facilitates a viewing that is dynamic" (Law, 2011, p. 374) and not constrained by Western fixed-point perspective.

There is an important ontological (philosophy of being) point underlying all this that pertains to how Daoist philosophers and artists understood their worlds as part of a harmonious "interconnected chain of things ... Rocks, trees, mountains, water, architecture and figures are all placed and structured in a continuous and ensuing flow," assisted by the changing perspectives (Law, 2011, p. 374) promoting "mind-travelling" around a colossal space that promotes a sense for the season rather than the particular day. The main idea is that Chinese scholars and artists place:

> an emphasis on a conceptual rather than visual manifestation of nature, ... to convey an experience of 'being in nature' rather than 'seeing nature.' This being in nature is not about any singular experience of when and where man encounters nature, but a perpetual truth experienced by people in/with nature, namely, the wholeness and universality of the cosmic, laws and cycles in nature, and the integrative harmony between man and things (Law, 2011, p. 378).

This tradition of painting "presents not a personal encounter with nature but rather a more generalized conceptual understanding of one's being *in/with nature*" (Law, 2011, p. 379). It is here that meaning and imagination meet as Coomaraswamy states: "'true knowledge of an object is not obtained by merely empirical observation or reflex registration ..., but only when the knower and known, seer and seen, meet in an act transcending distinction ...'" (Coomaraswamy, 1974, p. 6). The Daoist approach to art "serves as the stimulus to the release of spiritual awareness, of a kind of harmonious being between man and nature that goes beyond time and space" (Law, 2011, p. 381).

2.4 Summary

So, what have we learned about imagination from this diverse tour of disciplines and cultural perspectives? Aesthetic experience (1) *integrates sensory (stylistic) and semantic (narrative) information*, (2) *given the beholder's knowledge and relevant life* experiences, (3) *is shaped by setting and cultural background* (4) *within the constraints of bodily (i.e., neural) processes*, and (5) *emerges (Aktualgenese) over time to produce* (6) *representations (Vorstellungsgenese)* that are (7) dynamic and affective loaded (*Gefühlsgenese*). The more ambiguous the aesthetic work that we encounter, both perceptually and conceptually, the greater the room to enter into the work. On the one hand, we can project unresolved personal meanings onto the scene (a Western viewpoint), and, on the other hand, we can use the imagination as a vehicle for transcending the limitations of our own cultural understanding of the world (an Asian viewpoint).

Aesthetic imagination offers a reconciliation between *top-down* and *bottom-up* processing. Top-down processing is formal and involves analyzing paintings, literary works, or films by identifying the genre or style and comparing them with other works. A *bottom-up* approach focuses on the role of imagination in spontaneously shaping aesthetic experiences. John Dewey (1934) reminds us that "to perceive, a beholder must *create* his own experience. And his creation must include relations comparable to those which the original producer underwent." In this way, "emotionalized imagination" yields representations that emerge over time in perceptual, cognitive, and affective forms. Emotion is embedded in the very act of seeing. "There is, therefore, no such thing in perception as seeing or hearing *plus* emotion. The perceived object or scene is emotionally pervaded throughout." At the same time, "each of us assimilates to himself something of the values and meanings contained in past experiences" which determines the depth of aesthetic experience. This embodies the *web of personalized aesthetic experience.*

3 Scholarly Treatments of Imagination

It is indeed a challenge to build a unifying bridge among these creative and scholarly approaches, while being faithful to the topic of imagination in its different phases. A central point of Section 1 was that stability is an illusion and imagination manifests in every corner and moment of daily life: *What is not imagination, and does it exist*? Imagination lies hidden in the everyday assumptions of life. A fundamental contrast was drawn between instrumental problem-solving and expressing imagination emotionally in everyday life. The question arises as to whether we find this in history and across different cultures. At what point do scholars recognize the importance of unconscious influences and the role of self-awareness in creative acts? The answer may surprise readers.

In Section 2, I pointed out that aesthetic experience is founded on overcoming the "cognitive habit" of rushing to identify instrumental or meaningful content so as to experience the emergence of form from organized sensations. Creative people manipulate and organize these sensations; sounds, colours, textures, and movements, to provide an expressive context from which content emerges. The relationship of subject matter or content to an organized sensory background forms the metaphorical foundation of aesthetic beauty and experience. Cultural or aesthetic artifacts are created through the complementary involvement of the planful "Thinking-eye" and the expressive "Being-I." Aesthetic communication is successful when recipients intuit how a work unfolded for its creator and have a comparable experience. How early was this creative process appreciated in different societies representing Western and Eastern cultures?

3.1 Western Classical Imagination

We have scant opportunity here to contrast the restrained rationalism of an Apollonian approach with the more expressive Dionysian approach to aesthetics in Ancient Greek culture in general, and theatre in particular. Here is an example of what might be termed a Dionysian emotional dynamic that implicates the imagination. Phrynichus's play recalled the *Battle of Miletus* in 494 BCE in which the citizens suffered horribly at the hands of Persian troops. The historian Herodotus described how an audience in Athens burst into tears as the play forced them to re-experience the suffering of young and old citizens in Miletus, a city in Asia Minor tied to Athens. The audience was so traumatized that Phrynichus was fined 1,000 drachmas and ordered never to perform the play again. Their collective resonating to the experiences of the citizens of Miletus expresses an embodied "feeling cum perceiving cum imagining" that is foundational for immersion in the Greek aesthetic experience (Cupchik, Stamatopoulu, & Duan, 2021). This is consistent with Despina Stamatopoulou's description of the breadth of "mimesis" in Greek aesthetics linking rhythm, music, movement, emotions, and moral virtue to the likeness of character (Stamatopoulou & Cupchik, 2017).

The Greek philosophers Plato and Aristotle emphasized conscious thought and knowledge achieved through dialectic and logic, respectively. In Aristotle's linear model, sensation-imagination-reason, "*phantasia* is the intermediary between sensation and mind" (Cocking, 1991, p. 53). For Aristotle, imagination "'presents' the messages of the senses to the conscious mind as an 'appearance,' a unified picture" (Cocking, 1991, p. 270) which can then be recognized and labelled as a concept. An "important part of the imagination is the *sensus communis*, the 'common sense' which compares the particular senses of sight, hearing, taste, smell, touch, and combines them into the percept, the *aesthesis*, or *phantasia*. Such percepts may be present in the memory as images" (Cocking, 1991, p. 270). Aristotle also described a constructive or creative function of imagination which is to "break up perceptions into bits and put the bits together in different ways" (e.g., the centaur and the unicorn) (Cocking, 1991, p. 270) in a creative act. Not all imaginative activity necessarily leads to creative insight.

In an incisive analysis, Tateo (2017) describes Aristotle as a "theoretical empiricist" who conducted the equivalent of thought experiments based on a two-fold theory of mind. Accordingly, "whatever is in the intellect was originally in the senses; and there is no thinking without images (*phantasma*)" (p. 50). For Aristotle, "imagination is a motion that originates in sensation" creating images that become clearly defined with repetition and "constitute the objects of thinking" (p. 51). Imagination can also work the other way around, "from the inner mental work to external reality" as a "a form of preparation for action" that reflects "an appetite for something" (p. 51) and a readiness for action. Accordingly, images float between an experience of sensation from the outside world and internal arousal and needs. Like the model I described earlier, "imagination is generated by the real world and can generate action in return" (p. 51), serving as a halfway house between reality and fantasy. Both dimensions are implicated (see Figure 2), from external-internal or sensation-action (on the horizontal dimension) to conscious-unconscious (on the vertical dimension).

The Stoic Aetius tied the word *fancy* to "a vain impulse upon the mind of man, proceeding from nothing which is really imaginable; this is experienced in those that whirl about their idle hands and fight with shadows" (Cocking, 1991, p. 73). Coleridge adopted the same usage in nineteenth-century England. In contrast to the Greek Dionysian expressive treatment of *phantasia*, the Roman orator Cicero demonstrated the instrumental use of mnemonics by creating *imagines* (images) to be placed in an ordered system of *loci* (places) in a palace of the mind (Carraro et al., 2022). Each image was associated with a memory, thereby building a virtual palace within which to physically navigate one's reorganized past. The images are always in the same order, following a precise path of rooms, each with its own architecture (Cicero, 1949/1993). This strategy is well suited to a mechanical treatment of mimesis as the direct application of routinized motor responses to build an infrastructure of memory from which to retrace an oratorical work. These images in memory serve as a symbolic infrastructure exploited by Cicero as a tool for rhetoric.

In subsequent developments, the unconscious begins to take on a surprisingly important role, given that we generally consider it to be a modern concept. The Neoplatonist Plotinus (died AD 270) argued that *logos*, the intellectual principle, "can be at work in the human soul even when the soul is not conscious of it" (Cocking, 1991, p. 271). This extends to practical know-how which is associated with the imagination that may seem to have a magical quality because it refers to operations that cannot be rationally explained. Synesius of Cyrene (c. 378–430), addressing *phantasia*, described unconscious processes whereby problems could be solved while we sleep and are also the source of literary inspiration. We can appreciate the kind of speculative argumentation that is central to ancient forms of thinking. For Synesius, "phantasy" can embody our deepest desires in private images, for example, to free a prisoner or turn a private into a general. Subsequent developments opened the door for unconscious influences. Accordingly, unconscious and intuitive processes can spontaneously shape spiritual images.

Bundy (1927) points out that Augustine (AD 354–430) adopted a similar approach, arguing that the mind generates its own images rather than simply creating perceptual images out of passively received sensations (in Cocking, 1991, p. 72). Augustine introduced the word *imaginatio* as the equivalent of *phantasia.* He made a clear distinction between the simple sensory and the reproductive imagination in the absence of the object. His insight extends to hypothetical images of the Earth enclosed in a four-sided figure and even the schemata of thought, such as a concrete representation of the universe (Bundy, 1927, p. 160). The Ancients seem quite modern, as when Augustine describes "phantasies" that supplant true memory-images and appear to embody objective reality related to desire and aversion. He refers to "the fright of the man who cries out because he thinks he sees something, the physical effects of lascivious thoughts, our beguilements in sleep, the hallucinations of the mad, the visions of the prophet, and ordinary reverie" (Bundy, 1927, p. 162). While imagination can go beyond the capacities of simple reproductive memory "to make its own syntheses of sense-experience" (Cocking, 1991, p. 165), Augustine emphasized the "will" because people are responsible for their reactions to phantasies. He also stressed the importance of "intellectual vision" to bring imagination under control. While "Corporeal and spiritual visions may deceive us" (Cocking, 1991, p. 171), as when the "navigator thinks that the stars are moving, and that the oar in the water is broken," "intellectual vision never errs" (p. 171). Both the expressive and instrumental sides of imagination are evident here.

In his application of a "descriptive psychology" to the Medieval period, Bundy (1927) refers to an "empirical tradition" that is "interested in the orderly process of knowledge from percept to concept, and is also interested in the physiological conditions underlying thought" (p. 178) that reflects a "love of system, of careful analysis, of subtle distinctions, and precise subordination" (p. 178). The theory of imagination in this empirical tradition is associated with "the so-called faculty psychologies, wherein each mental power is assigned to its proper cell or ventricle in the head according to its function in an orderly process of cognition from the first sensation to the idea" (Bundy, 1927, p. 179). The seeds of neuroscience and faculty psychology are evident here.

From a Christian religious perspective, there is also a spiritual side to the story in the "theology of emanation" of Plotinus where images derived from mysticism, take on an intense sensory quality. This pertains to the symbolic "contents of imagination." The use of imagery to represent the path to mystical union is very strong in St. John of the Cross' *Ascent of Mount Carmel,* as well as fellow Carmelite St. Theresa of Avila's *Interior Castle*. A systematized, widely practiced use of imagination in the Catholic West is St. Ignatius of Loyola's "imaginative prayer" in the *Spiritual Exercises* (Jesuits). "Christians, early and modern, have acknowledged the importance of imagination in apprehending the *Logos*. Allegory is a clear example, though perhaps even more explicitly, Ignatius Loyola (trans. 2015) advised the faithful to engage in *imaginative prayer* – a practice that involves imagining oneself situated in a scene, such as the foot of the Cross, in vivid detail, empathetically engaged and in search of grace" (Boulis et al., 2023, p. 112). Michelle Karnes (2011) offers a detailed exploration of medieval gospel meditations as acts of imagination presuming a cognitive faculty "that enables the mind to apprehend truth" (p. 21).

A different approach to imagination is incorporated into the Jewish Chassidic tradition of spiritual elevation and social engagement that is more focused on "acts of imagination." Susan Handelman (1982) addresses the role of "reality," rather than literal "substance," in her study of Jewish thought with a movement "towards a structural or processual rather than substantial approach to reality" (p. 35). "The Rabbinic tendency ... is towards differentiation, metaphorical simplicity, multiple meaning. One needs to search the forms, shapes, patterns of words, and their varying connections within an expansive text; there is no confinement of meaning within the ontology of substance" (Handelman, 1982, p. 33). Accordingly, "the particular and concrete take precedence over the general and abstract" with the fundamental view that "all is interconnected and interrelated" as part of "a continuous and unified process" (Handelman, 1982, p. 39). This gives rise to the inference that a text and the rules that govern interpretation are part of a unified process. Handelman cites Adir Steinsaltz's comment that "Jewish thought uses pictorial or imagery concepts instead of abstract concepts" (p. 61). Metonymy, rather than metaphor, aptly characterizes this effort to grasp "the inner reality of the thing" (Handelman, 1982, p. 62). This movement away from the literal, which can extend to treating dependent measures as if they were objectively "real," lies at the heart of my unending search for meaningful process underlying the "family resemblance" of words related to imagination. One feels the meaning underlying the principles articulated in Section 4 before one can articulate them.

3.1.1 Summary

We can see in the early European treatment of imagination that a linear or serial model is favoured, moving from sensation to thought through the mediating role of a synthesizing "common sense" imagination. While there is a legitimate concern for errors of judgment, an avenue is provided for novel syntheses and even heightened spiritual experiences via imagination. This "descriptive" approach to imagination extrapolates meaning from the experiences of scholars in everyday life. An expressive approach is evident in Greek poetics, while Cicero exemplifies the application of an instrumental and logical use of images to foster memory in the Latin tradition. A further contrast can be drawn between religious traditions that treat words literally as if they were substance (Christian) versus as allusions to hidden processes (Jewish). The Chinese Taoist tradition must of course be considered, and it will be shortly.

3.2 A Humanist Perspective

The full expression of imagination starts in the nineteenth century with historians, poets, philosophers, literary theorists, and psychologists of different stripes. Lyell's (1990) *Principles of Geology* introduced the idea that the physical world evolved slowly, a theme adopted by Charles Darwin in his principles of evolution with an emphasis on the survival of the fittest. This led to the idea of the layered self that has agency and evolves over time. One might say that the existential movement emerged from self-awareness and an interest in human memory. George Poulet (1950/1956) considers this idea of "experienced continuity" to be a great development of the eighteenth century. Following in the tradition of Rousseau "all at once the mind is able to feel an entire past reborn within itself" (Poulet, 1950/1956, p. 27). This approach emphasizes "an identity of nature in all men, but also an identity of person" (Poulet, 1950/1956, p. 30) and leads to "the *intuition of becoming* . . . which is always future . . . [and] *come*[s] *out of the depths of time*" (pp. 31–32). An emphasis on duration is also evident in Bergson, as we discover ourselves in the depths of "total memory that is always on the very verge of consciousness" (Poulet, 1950/1956, p. 34). The implication of all this, leading into the twentieth century, is that in "Every instant one acts" and thereby "one creates oneself and the world" (Poulet, 1950/1956, p. 35) which is the essence of existential thought.

Imagination, as a living process, is embodied in the contrasting views of scholars who were also creatives and reflected on the process. The critical point is that they built a bridge between artifacts or creative products and the worlds of playwrights or poets and audiences. The same question can be asked in the West as to whether we are detached from the work or deeply embedded in it. The central comparison in Western culture is between British Enlightenment theory as well as French Neoclassicism and German Romanticism. Whereas the English tradition was more purpose-oriented and instrumental, the German tradition favoured spontaneity and soulful initiative in approaching theatrical dramas. In contrast to Schiller's "play drive," Samuel Taylor Coleridge (1772–1834) described the experience of aesthetic illusion as the product of a "willing suspension of disbelief for the moment, which constitutes poetic faith" (Coleridge, *Biographia Literaria*, 1817/1983, cited in Burwick, 1991, p. 221). A familiar modern contrast would be between Method Acting, in which performers access personal experiences as a vehicle for expressing their character's life situation, and a Classical approach that uses studied gestures to embody and convey standardized social meanings.

It is worthwhile reviewing how imagination is shaped in these more modern illustrations of the Ancient Greek Apollonian (British and French) and Dionysian (German) accounts of theatrical experience. A critical point here is that their implicit accounts of imaginative processes are grounded in relations between creatives or recipients of theatrical experiences. The British and French approaches favoured a detachment of the audience from the work that, in essence, manipulates their imaginative experiences and surface feelings of pleasure and excitement from the outside. The German Romantic approach emphasized the more intimate relationship between audiences who find personal meaning in situations described in works that move them emotionally. In this next section, I spell out in greater detail these underlying dynamics.

3.2.1 British Enlightenment and French Neoclassicism

In the "Enlightened" British tradition of "mimesis" (copying or representation), the aesthetic focus was on a kind of "disinterested" pleasure or enjoyment of something for its own sake (hence, intrinsic) as opposed to a pragmatic motivation. For Frances Hutcheson (1694–1746) the discerning of "uniformity amidst variety" involved a special sense or faculty (taste), a special criterion, and a resulting *disinterested* pleasure (Hutcheson, 1725/2004). Hutcheson's principle of "uniformity amidst variety" involved a special sense or faculty (taste), a special criterion, and a resulting *disinterested* pleasure that reflected a practised eye, enhanced by cultural experience. The Enlightenment approach to theatre emphasized *manipulating* an audience's imagination and emotions which could be accomplished by choosing culturally shared subject matter so that observers did not need specialized knowledge to appreciate the work. In this context, familiarity was essential so that strict *mimesis,* the controlled "imitation of nature" ("as if it were the thing itself") would link a person with the familiar world (Schneider, 1995, p. 83). Because events on the stage appear *real*, spectators would experience an involuntary emotional response that overwhelms reason, and willfully submit to the illusion (Burwick, 1991). This approach to illusion in theatre presumes a *passive* response "in sympathy with increasing emotional stimulation until the reason surrenders to the force of the passions" (Burwick, 1991, p. 222).

In a similar manner, the French Neoclassical tradition emphasized the role of the "three unities" of time, place, and action in shaping dramatic illusion (Burwick, 1991). Denis Diderot (1713–1784), reflected on the circumstances that shape illusion, specifically the paradoxical behaviour of actors who exhibit passion while maintaining total self-control. The greater the self-control of the actor, the more involuntary the emotional response of the audience member who is overcome by the performance. In accordance with the Enlightenment belief in *mimesis* as the embodiment of causality, everything on stage must unfold as if it were real and following rational laws. Simulation and likeness are sufficient to evoke feelings and emotions in the imagination of receptive audience members.

The same approach could be applied to the role of "mimesis" or simulation in the Neoclassical approach to painting (Fried, 1980). Diderot described the responsibility of artists to pick a single moment in time when characters are most *absorbed* in a meaningful activity which creates "an illusion of the inherent dynamism, directedness, and compulsive force of causation itself" (Fried, 1980, p. 85). This presumed an instantaneous recognition of "the *tableau*, the portable and self-sufficient picture that could be taken in at a glance" (Fried, 1980, p. 89). The figures must be absorbed in the action and appear unaware of its effects on the audience. This fits with Lord Shaftsbury's notion of "Tablature, when the work is in reality 'a single piece, comprehended in one view, and formed according to one single intelligence, meaning, or design; which constitutes a real whole'" (Fried, 1980, p. 89). The goal of painting then is to attract, arrest, and enthral the beholder. Ironically, Fried underscored the paradox of having a painting that attracts the beholder "in a perfect trance of involvement" while, at the same time, "negating the beholder's presence" (Fried, 1980, p. 103). The emphasis was on simulating "real" events in accordance with a rational model of causality that could manipulate audience experience so that spectators of theatre or paintings could appraise it as legitimate or accurate. This fits with an empiricist belief system moving from sensation to perception and cognition in a linear, deductive fashion.

3.2.2 German Romanticism

For a German perspective on becoming and growth, we turn to Wolfgang von Goethe (1749–1832), the great writer and scientist who founded the field of plant morphology predicated on the idea of unfolding growth from seed to plant. He embodied the "poetics of science" and the importance of shifting between an engaged viewpoint of phenomena in the world, both physical and social, and scientific detachment which lies at the foundation of orderly experimentation. Ernst Cassirer (1950) points out Goethe's relations to evolutionary theory and his appreciation of the "intermingling of being and becoming, of permanence and change" (p. 139). He treated "the synthetic work of the imagination" with "the analytical work of the concept" (Cassirer, 1950, p. 143) in a complementary way. Central to his approach was balancing the "particular" and the "universal," part and whole, such that "they interpenetrate one another" (Cassirer, 1950, p. 145). Goethe, the poet, and his playwriting friend Friedrich Schiller (1759–1805) embodied George Poulet's (1950/1956) "romanticism of experienced continuity" and the "intuition of becoming" (p. 31). This captures the modern challenge of the need to experience continuity in the midst of uncertainty and tension. In essence, imagination provides the glue. To that end, Schiller (1759–1805) described a "play drive" (*Spieltrieb*), related to "aesthetic education," which helps unify perceptual, cognitive, and affective aspects of experience (Schiller, 1965/1794).

The Romantic view emphasized integrating sensual perception with an evolving self in the light of life's contradictions. Schiller described the personal experiences of audience members, combining their "own sensual and intellectual drives" (Burwick, 1991, p. 15). The aesthetic experience could bridge the sensuous and the moral in that tragedy could elicit sympathy for the characters. Johann Elias Schlegel (1719–1749) believed that art and theatre should balance the subject matter and the order or style. If the subject matter evokes excessively strong emotion that seizes the imagination, then the hidden order cannot be discerned, and this diminishes the value of the work. Theatre should reflect the situations and historical traditions that are meaningful to audiences and thereby enhance their social awareness. He opposed the British idea of tricking the spectator into believing that the event on the stage is real through the use of "crude naturalism with intent to deceive" (Wilkinson, 1945, p. 78). The goal should therefore be to provide a meaningful context and lend coherence to the audience's experience; the *unity of action* is more important than the unities of time and place.

August Schlegel (1767–1845), Johann's nephew, focussed on processes underlying audience experiences and grounded "aesthetic illusion in imagination" (Burwick, 1991, p. 193), treating it as a "waking dream, to which we voluntarily surrender ourselves" (Burwick, 1991, p. 194). For Schlegel, reality and illusion actually coexist; "The reality of the dramatic dialogue is that the text is written; the illusion is that dramatic dialogue is spoken spontaneously" (Burwick, 1991, p. 201). The goal in theatre is not merely to present a causal chain but, instead, "the ordering of human action into a unique aesthetic experience" (Burwick, 1991, p. 155). Shakespeare's ability to present fundamental conflicts of everyday life in a way that could resonate with personal experiences of audience members was very appealing to him and he was the first scholar to translate Shakespeare's plays into German. In sum, writers of the Romantic era recreated situations that were multilayered, embodying socially meaningful events filled with unresolved tensions and conflicts. Audiences could relate to these scenes by using imagination and emotions to bring unity to the experience. Their familiarity with the situations and accessing of relevant life experiences lent a dynamic closure to the aesthetic experience.

3.2.3 Parallels in Chinese Aesthetic Theory

There is an interesting parallel between German Romanticism and ideas in Classical Chinese aesthetic theory related to both poetry and painting. While both perspectives describe how people are embedded in nature, Romanticism stresses projection or a resonance between internal stress and chaotic aspects of nature. Chinese aesthetic theory places a greater emphasis on "emptiness" and calm along with the value of immersing oneself in nature. It is worthwhile taking a brief detour into Chinese aesthetics because it addresses a distinctive approach to imaginative engagement with nature. There is a clear contrast between a Western emphasis on the human separation from an empirical nature and a Chinese account of being embedded in nature. The Western approach leads to careful predictions about future events, whereas the ancient Chinese approach values the calm that comes from transcendent consciousness.

In relation to literary criticism, Liu Hsieh (c. AD 465–522) states that "the critic should be able through imagination to trace back from the words to the feeling of the author" and thereby "grasp the meaning or the esthetic beauty of a literary work" (Liu, 2015, p. xl). Accordingly, "Genius operates through imagination, the power of association of ideas, and the ability to forge metaphors" (p. xlv). Writing during the Classical period, he refers to the "mystic subtlety of the imagination" and the role played by "vacancy and tranquility . . . in the development of literary thinking" (p. lii). In his discussion of painting, Sirén (1935/2005) reminds us that "The Taoist conception of real knowledge or insight" involves "an identity between the knower and the known" (p. 25). This sense of "spirit-resonance" happens "when the mind has been cleansed of all beclouding thoughts and attuned to the silent music that accompanies every manifestation of life" (p. 107). Thus, in contrast to European painting, "Space was not . . . a cubic volume that could be geometrically constructed, it was something illimitable and incalculable which might be, to some extent, suggested by the relation of forms to tonal values but which always extended beyond every material indication and carried a suggestion of the infinite" (p. 97).

David Hinton, the American poet and translator of Chinese texts, treats Taoism as a "spiritual ecology" (Hinton, 2012), with deep ontological implications, so that "presence" and "absence" are complementary concepts, one flowing into the other. He points out that, in contrast, Paleolithic artists in Western culture "began to push things outside themselves, objectifying them, and thereby opening the distinction between self-identity and landscape" (Hinton, 2012, p. 39). Herein lies a fundamental distinction between Chinese and Western ontologies, concerns about what is real. In Western cave paintings, the world becomes a separate entity contrasting with the self. In a Taoist approach to painting, the self merges with the landscape in what might be described as a transcendent aesthetic action (Magon & Cupchik, 2023). And yet the pictographic quality of ancient Chinese characters invites immediate experience in the same way that images on cave walls foster immediate perceptual experience. The value of pursing Hinton's account of an "archeology of mind" (Hinton, 2012, p. 56) lies in our appreciating how "images from the observable universe" help to create the mind "through a complex process of metaphoric transference" . . . "from the empirical Cosmos" (p. 56). If the reader finds these words to be challenging, so do I. And, yet, deep insight lies therein about how sensation transforms into knowledge through the mediating role of imagination.

The ambiguity of poetic texts and the empty spaces in images invite a "meditative experience" (Hinton, 2013) in both readers and viewers. This is fostered by different kinds of techniques related to "Mysterious utterances, misty terminology, fragmentary collage form with open and enigmatic juxtapositions, an abounding ambiguity that exploits the uncertainty inherent in the syntax and semantics of ancient Chinese . . . " (p. 22). It is in Chinese landscape paintings that we find: "the pregnant emptiness of Absence, and the landscape of Presence as it burgeons forth from Absence in a perpetual process of transformation" (p. 29). While this flow of complementarities, between Presence and Absence, may sound alien to a Western mind used to foregrounds and backgrounds, stimulus and response, these are precisely the conditions of ambiguity and uncertainty that invite imagination.

3.2.4 From Humanism to Experimental Psychology

The contrast between humanism and the emerging experimental psychology is noteworthy. For an in-depth account of richness in imaginative creative processes, it is important to spend some time reading humanist scholars whose "ecological validity" is founded on an in-depth exploration of individual works and their authors in a historical context. Burwick (1991) describes how "dramatic illusion depends on the engagement of the imagination" in combination with the emotions. From the perspective of Burwick and Pape (1990), a "new concept of reality . . . emerged in the age of the Enlightenment, a new social function of literature . . . to regulate human and social development" (p. 2). Indeed, they go so far as to comment on how the theatre of the laboratory shapes the experiences of participants. According to Pfeiffer (1990), "Empiricism is concerned . . . with the control of the conditions under which the negotiation, production, and often the 'staging' of what may be called various realities and fictions take place" (p. 94). Indeed, one should turn to Iser (1993) whose literary anthropology addresses relations between "the fictive and the imaginary" in relation to a "fictionalizing act."

One can only imagine conversations between humanist scholars of literature and psychologists where the challenges of richness and precision would indeed play out. This would not be a peaceful conversation. Humanists explore in-depth the "ecological validity" of artistic and theatrical works in relation to the "lived world" of cultural experiences. It is challenging to link their abstract concepts of "aesthetic illusion" and the "imaginary," and the cultural conditions in which they are situated, as acts of imagination in everyday and aesthetic life, with concrete and operationalized psychological ideas related to "images" or "illusions" as contents of imagination.

3.3 Nineteenth-Century Thoughts about Culture and Science

Theory development in the nineteenth century balanced the rationalism of the Enlightenment with the irrationalism of Romanticism. In his review of developments in the history of "dynamic psychiatry," Henri Ellenberger (1970) points out that the Enlightenment "proclaimed the values of reason and society," whereas "Romanticism had the cult of the irrational and of the individual" (p. 199). The philosopher Ernst Cassirer (1950) reminds us that Goethe was both a Romantic author and philosopher, as well as a forerunner of evolutionary theory, who described the "intermingling of being and becoming, of permanence and change" (p. 139) as well as the need to see "the eternal in the transitory" (p. 147). Accordingly, he was able to balance "the analytical work of the concept" with "the synthetic work of the imagination" (p. 143).

Wilhelm Dilthey's (1833–1911) contrast of the "human sciences" and "natural sciences" formalizes differences between Romanticism and the Enlightenment. His "human science" approach encompassed the humanities and the social sciences, including psychology, political sciences, as well as philology, literary and cultural studies. From a holistic perspective regarding "lived-experience," the "whole self" engages with personally and culturally meaningful situations and the "structured mind" unifies cognition, affection, and conation (action). In addition, a deeper understanding of lived-experience and culture requires reflective self-awareness. The poet imaginatively transforms the images and qualities of everyday experience to heighten experiences and interpretation is central to understanding cultural phenomena. In contrast, the "natural sciences" focus on "knowledge" wherein hypothesis, prediction, and causal models explain physical phenomena. Treating the mind as if it were a physical phenomenon is central to the development of behavioural-cognitive psychology, in contrast to the humanist tradition. Herein lies the problem when abstract processes are operationalized, and sometimes confused with, concrete laboratory-based measures.

3.3.1 Embodied Imagination: The Organic and Temporal Arc in Gestalt Psychology

The idea of a layered self was established in the eighteenth and nineteenth centuries. This was complemented by interactions between people and the everyday or aesthetic worlds. Two complementary themes that underlie their interactions involve instrumental attempts at survival and expressive efforts after meaning. The ideas of Goethe, Darwin, and Dilthey are central to the organic and temporal arcs that are embodied in imagination. The idea of an evolving self applies both to a seed that turns into a mature plant and people who grow from childhood to maturity. While both plants and people are subject to environmental pressures, the role of evolving cognition and self-awareness is crucial to the process. Another related concept from Gestalt psychology is that "the objects we perceive are always located in what would now be called self-organizing systems – constantly changing dynamic contexts or situations, of which our phenomenal selves, too, are parts" (Ash, 1998, p. 2). From Dewey's (1934) pragmatic or functional approach to psychology, the process "continues until a mutual adaptation of the self and object emerges and that particular experience comes to a close" (p. 44). Imagination plays a central role in adaptation as we try to become clear about the meaning of a situation and our position within it. This reminds me of the role of "common sense" in Aristotle's linear model linking sensation and belief in the world of experience.

This microgenetic approach in Gestalt psychology describes stages in the emergence of perception in which imagination plays an important role as processing unfolds in real time. For Werner and Kaplan (1963), the earliest stage of perception has "an affective-sensory-motor nature" in which representations embody "personal, idiomatic, and contextualized gestures or images" and the movement is toward "a progressive differentiation and articulation of connotations ... and a progressive channeling of meanings towards communally adequate verbal forms" (p. 242). Similarly, from the perspective of a cognitive approach to visual perception, Neisser (1967) argued that "contours are not simply 'registered,' but must be actively constructed, which takes time" (Neisser, 1967, p. 26). The link with Ancient Greek theory is clear as perception moves from sensation to reason through the mediation of organizing processes. In modern treatment, global sensory processes lead to formal identity (i.e., reason) as the process becomes more articulated.

Ernst Kris (1952) describes the complementary roles of unconscious (bottom-up) and conscious (top-down) processes in a biphasic process where "inspiration" is followed by "elaboration." The bottom-up inspirational stage has access to primary process thinking which is not bound by logic and is free from the traditional constraints of time and space, while top-down elaboration is governed by secondary process thinking which is logical and reality bound. Kris introduces the concept of *regression-in-service-of-the-ego* whereby the syncretic images offered by the unconscious are sought out and then manipulated within the framework of artistic design. Accordingly, ambiguities inherent in paintings may stimulate imaginal, emotional and empathic responses in viewers who *unconsciously* recognize personally meaningful themes. In a poetic context, "Metaphor serves as a stimulus to functional regression because the primary process itself is metaphoric and imagistic" (Kris, 1952, p. 258). Imagination is spurred by unconscious activities.

According to Rudolf Arnheim's (1904–2007) holistic Gestalt approach, aesthetic reception processing unfolds in a *bottom-up* manner from *global* to *differentiated* or *articulated*. He argued that people discern expressive qualities of artworks directly without being explicitly aware of the specific underlying structural features. Following ideas from field theory," the "priority of physiognomic properties should not come as a surprise" (p. 430) because "expression is a configuration of forces" (p. 434) and "an inherent characteristic of perceptual patterns" (p. 433). Arnheim assumed that "expression has its origin in the perceived pattern and in the reaction of the brain field of vision to this pattern" (p. 434) and, since this pattern "arouses a corresponding configuration of forces, the observer's reaction is more than a mere taking cognizance of an outer object" (p. 437). It is founded on an implicit awareness of the body's own reactions to structured events in the external world and, accordingly, the body "feels" the painting before it "knows" it. People have a natural disposition to resolve this ambiguity and the resulting tension energizes the process. The metaphors embedded in artistic works "make the reader penetrate the concrete shell of the world of things by combination of objects that have little in common but the underlying pattern" (Arnheim, 1971, pp. 435–436). This lies at the heart of acts of imagination.

Wolfgang Iser (1978) brings the contrast between instrumental and expressive imagination together when addressing the challenges posed by language in expository and fictional texts. In expository texts, the goal is to narrow down the multiplicity of potential meanings by ensuring that textual segments are connected. Fictional texts differ by breaking down "*good continuation*" (a Gestalt principle) through the introduction of "blanks" or empty spaces in the unfolding narrative. This lack of fluency in the text automatically mobilizes readers to engage in "acts of consistency-building" (p. 185) and "image-building" (p. 187). For Iser (1993) the literary text "functions to bring into view the interplay among the fictive, the real, and the imaginary" (p. 3). While the nuances underlying Iser's "literary anthropology," go beyond the limits of this Element, the process involves an act of imaginative construction of felt meanings.

Suffice it to say that humanist scholars deconstruct language in relation to cultural products, both visual and literary. They have closely addressed relations between products and the artists or writers who created them. It would be ideal if empirical psychologists invested the same effort to follow Danziger's advice and search for hidden meanings in "conceptual variables." When we appreciate that "Experimental outcomes are artifacts, not natural phenomena" (p. 187) and that "*Methodology is not ontologically neutral*" (Danziger, 2000, p. 332), it becomes apparent that data alone will not resolve differences among theories whose origins can be traced back over several centuries. To better understand processes underlying different phases of imagination, it would be ideal to reflect on relations between social and cultural phenomena in the world and the methods we use to study them. In this way, our concepts would be grounded in real-world phenomena rather than the measures upon which they are based.

3.4 The Depth of Imagination

The depth dimension implicates imagination in two ways. First, the preservation of material from earlier stages of life tends to be syncretic or fragmented. Second, these fragmented elements tend to have emotional associations and the more powerful negative ones tend to be repressed, emerging transformed in dreams. While focusing on art, Ehrenzweig's (1967) model of attention has broader value. In accordance with an organic treatment of imagination, he described "an undifferentiated attention akin to syncretistic vision which does not focus on detail, but holds the total structure of the work of art in a single undifferentiated view" (p. 23). For Ehrenzweig (1967), unconscious perception and vision are sufficiently undifferentiated so that figure/ground boundaries become obscure. Thus, "outer perception and inner phantasy become indistinguishable" (Ehrenzweig, 1967, p. 272) such that "image-making" yields a "type of imagery which is outward perception and inward directed phantasy at the same time" (pp. 272–273). At this syncretic level of functioning, any "objects, however different in shape or outline, can become fully equated with each other" (p. 272). The artist Paul Klee described this as "dispersed attention." It is here that the "Becoming-I" selects meaningful elements to incorporate in a work in accordance with the trained discipline of the "Thinking-eye" (Cupchik, 2016).

Henri Ellenberger (1970) briefly comments on the "old concept of 'imagination'" in his discussion of the "First Dynamic Psychiatry" (p. 111) in relation to the concept of *imaginatio*, a term that he describes as a "power of the mind." From a pragmatic viewpoint, he cites the work of Montaigne who associated it with physical manifestations such as mental disease and even stigmata. Concerned about the "*Power of Human Imagination*," in the eighteenth century, Muratori wrote about manifestations of imagination in dreams, visions, delusions, fixed ideas, and even somnambulism that became a focal point. Consistent with my earlier emphasis on real-world events, somnambulism became a popular topic and this lead, naturally, to an interest in "fluidity" and hypnotism. Of course, an emphasis was placed on the royal road to the unconscious. This leads naturally to processes underlying dreams whereby repressed childhood memories, embedded in the "latent content" of the unconscious, gain access to the "manifest content" of the recalled dream. "Dream work" transforms the "latent content," neutralizing deeper emotionally loaded meanings through mechanisms such as displacement, condensation, symbolization, and dramatization (see the "dream work" figure on page 491).

Hans and Shulamith Kreitler (1972) also addressed the complex nature of multileveled aesthetic works within a Gestalt framework. "Multileveledness is the capacity of a work to be grasped, elaborated, and experienced in several systems of connected potential meanings, each of which allows a meaningful, clear, comprehensive, and sometimes even autonomous organization of all the major constituents of the work of art" (pp. 294–295). Each of the levels in a narrative "affords a view of the whole" (p. 297) in terms of which the work is understood. The Kreitlers incorporated a psychodynamic viewpoint, arguing that "*a major motivation for art is tensions which exist in the spectator of art prior to his exposure to the work of art. The work of art mediates the relief of these preexisting tensions by generating new tensions which are specific*" (p. 19). Gestalt psychologists emphasize tension and its resolution both in the artwork and the viewer, a focus that reaches back to the Romantics and traverses the boundaries between Gestalt psychology, behaviourism, and psychodynamics.

Albert Rothenberg (1988, 1990) has similarly examined the dynamic quality of the layers of meaning for stimulating creative thought. He explored the concept of layering (Rothenberg, 1976, 1979, 1986) in a series of studies on the "homospatial" process with "*two or more discrete entities occupying the same space, a conception leading to the articulation of new identities*" (Rothenberg, 1990, p. 25). Creative authors and artists can bring separated elements together in novel ways. The "creative person separates out critical aspects of the material he works with, and he fuses or brings these separated elements together" (Rothenberg, 1990, p. 128). It was this interplay of concrete material elements that so engaged highly creative authors and artists interviewed by Rothenberg (1990).

3.5 Cognitive/Behavioral Approaches

A visit to Anna Abraham's *Handbook of the Imagination* (2020) provides an ample sample space of chapters in the cognitive/behavioural tradition. One thing that stands out is a tendency to what might be called theoretical reductionism by which I mean a disposition to frame processes related to imagination in terms of pre-existing fundamental categories in psychology. Accordingly, a "unified theory of imagination" involves representational content that balances episodic and semantic elements in accordance with task demands (Irish, 2020). This approach fits in a space that is forward-looking and conscious so that hypothetical thinking (Ball, 2020) "involves imagining possibilities and exploring their consequences through a process of mental simulation" (p. 514) with a focus on cause-and-effect relationships. Related to this is research on the impact of "imagined alternatives on moral causal influences" in relation to counterfactual thinking and inferences about intentions (Byrne, 2020). In his account of the role played by imagination in aesthetic experience, Vartanian (2020) discusses a "search for meaning" along with a preference for authenticity and "internally generated thoughts" (p. 586).

3.6 Sociocultural Approaches

The sociocultural approach does not treat people as processing their worlds in isolation from social worlds. Rather, it "aims at capturing the 'cultural' nature of human experience" (Zittoun, Glaveanu, & Hawlina, 2020, p. 143) and stresses the "mutual constitution between mind and culture, psychological functions, and their material contexts" (p. 145). As a consequence, it is essential to study persons in social contexts, and all variations of time, including the evolution of species and societies, along with all cultural resources (see p. 145). Following Vygotsky, they associate the development of imagination with that of language and related conceptual systems. Imagination is "culturally constructed" (p. 146) so people can "temporarily disengage" from immediate situations in socially shared reality. Imagination is a "form of experiencing through meaningful scenarios" (Tateo, 2017).

The creative potential of imagination is founded on its being both associative and combinatorial to consider other possible worlds. Of great importance is the potential to decouple from "the here and now of socially shared experience" (p. 152) when triggered by an event. Looking backward in time, Shanks (2020) describes how the "archeological imagination frames our engagement with remains of the past, frames our perception of the past, frames the possibility of making sense of the past" (p. 48). A value is placed on treating "identities as constantly reimagined, reperformed, recreated, distributed through ongoing experiences, engagements, relationships, assemblages of people, and all manner of things" (p. 60).

Social constructionists explore the diverse manifestations of imagination as "firmly rooted in the human body" so that "past, present, and future are closely interwoven" and "create the human world" (Wulf, 2022, p. 3). The images that people create are used to "interpret the world" (p. 5) in its diversity. The collected images are expressed in "practices of the body" (p. 7) via play and dance. The breath and diversity of images are also underscored as graphic, optical, perceptual, mental, and verbal. The image offers a "portrayal and expression of imagination" (p.60) and meditating on symbolically rich images can foster human spiritual development (p. 71). This even extends to imaginary objects the boundaries of which may elude the individual (p. 105).

3.7 Neuroscience Perspectives

Neuroscience researchers have become keenly interested in the creative imagination, particularly as it pertains to innovation. Their work has been driven by the idea of "remote association" (Mednick, 1962). Functional magnetic resonance imaging (fMRI) has been used to assess the dynamic interactions among various brain regions in different cortical networks that mediate both spontaneous and controlled cognitive processes. Attention has been given to different Networks that might play pivotal roles, including relations between the default mode network (DMN), the cognitive control network (CCN), and the salience network (SN). The DMN, encompassing cortical structures in the temporal, parietal, and frontal cortex, is an area of the brain found to be typically more active when test subjects are not engaged in a task (i.e., when they are "mind wandering"). The CCN, encompassing cortical structures in the prefrontal and parietal cortex, tends to be more active when subjects require focused attention to perform a particular task, or when they switch between tasks. The SN affords flexibility depending upon the challenge, which can contrast instrumental and expressive forms of creative imagination.

The psychological aspect of creative imagination can be integrated with the neuroscience approach. A process known as "leaky sensory gating" enables creative individuals to access ideas outside their immediate attention. The pivotal idea is that creative individuals demonstrate a rapid shift between activating the DMN and other networks such as the CCN. This rapid "flipping" (turning the DMN on and off) reflects a shift between global monitoring (i.e., waiting for something meaningful to happen) and focused attention to salient information. Critically, since creativity may rely on both "leaky" and focused attention, dynamic interactions between these networks and the limbic system will be important in theoretical development.

We have established that Brodmann area 10 in the brain plays a crucial role in orienting participants to adopt an "aesthetic attitude" (Cupchik et al., 2009). In addition, Brodmann area 7 offers a distinction between hard and soft-edge images. Wölfflin (1915/1950) has similarly described "linear" (hard) versus "painterly" (soft) as a fundamental dimension underlying the structure of Western art. The "painterly" (i.e., soft-edge) qualities of a visual image are sufficiently ambiguous as to invite a viewer to project meaning onto it. Our recently completed study (Vartanian et al., 2024) examined the neural structures underlying *instrumental* (i.e., goal-oriented) versus *expressive* (*i.e., experience*-oriented) interactions with visual images in a story telling task. Our goal is to address neural structures underlying creative imagination relating the DMN to instrumental and expressive imaginative creativity. The DMN will be related to the CCN when the executive function solves a problem and to the limbic system when past experience shapes an emerging novel image. In reviewing the highlights of the now completed study, we found that reduced frontal control over the default mode network facilitates expressive imagination for story generation, via minimization of control processes that limit mind wandering and internally generated cognition. A complete presentation of the findings requires more space than allotted here.

3.8 Conclusions

We generally believe that science has progressed beyond ancient knowledge and that we are closer to understanding imagination, The substance of this section suggests that this is an illusion at best or perhaps even a delusion that expresses "modernity." What is the argument behind my conclusion? I proposed at the outset that instrumental actions fostering survival in all species should be contrasted with an "effort after meaning" that is predicated on language. Our data show that these complementary aspects of imagination are present in students from China, North America, and European cultures today. Indeed, we can trace this development in the Apollonian (rational) and Dionysian (emotional) aspects of Greek culture as well as in the Confucian (rational) and Taoist (transcendent) sides of Chinese culture. Aristotle's linear model, incorporating sensation, imagination (the "common sense"), and rational mind carries through thinking of The Enlightenment, and is reflected in the metatheory of cognitive behaviourism today. The expressive side of imagination is revealed in theorizing and descriptions of irrational and unconscious activity in the first centuries CE and then is embodied in German Romanticism, and the psychoanalytic and Gestalt movements.

Neuroscience has provided a modern account of areas in the brain that orient us to aesthetic experience and to address meanings hidden in soft-edge images, not to speak of a default mode network (DMN) that frees us to explore beyond the constraints of sensations at the moment. Chinese culture has embraced our intimate relations with nature in contrast to a Western emphasis on separation and control. Indeed, the complementary themes of explanation/prediction (natural science) and understanding (human science) underscore the continuous presence of instrumental and expressive themes in our lives. As time unfolded, the boundaries between disciplines became more salient. Humanist scholars explore nuanced meanings embedded both in creative works and in the cultural settings that shaped the creative people who produced them. Scientists have been more focused on solving material problems by exploring the physical boundaries of our world and engaging in predictions.

4 Toward a Phase Theory of Imagination

A unified theory of imagination must be sensitive to lessons learned from different cultures over the span of time. The strategy adopted here has been to present ideas related to how imagination impacts everyday life, as well as aesthetic episodes of creation or reception, given what scholars have proposed in Western and Eastern scholarship. In this section, I review the insights of great scholars, while at the same time trying to draw out a set of unifying principles that link everyday life and aesthetics experiences associated with both creation and reception.

4.1 Principle: The Web of Imagination

Imagination has historically been treated as a "faculty" with a possible location in the brain, though it did not make it to Spurzheim's list of "intellectual faculties" related to phrenology (Boring, 1950, p. 55). This is an ironic nineteenth-century failure! I am following Boussac's advice to avoid an "ontological trap" by treating imagination as a thing, and Danziger's assertion that concepts in psychology represent different discursive communities. Accordingly, *Imagination is like a web encompassing sensation, meaning, memory, emotion, and bodily states in a unified experience against the background of culture and society.*

4.2 Principle: Imaginative Processes Appear in Different Phases

The approach proposed in this Element treats concepts related to imagination as different *phases* of a common underlying process. Accordingly, words like image, imaginative, imaginary, imagery, imagine, reimagine, and so forth, refer to different aspects of a common process linking a representation with sensation (external or internal) in a social context. Different approaches in the humanities and the sciences favour one or another of these and related terms. Some focus on the *contents* of imagination which can be more concrete (images, illusions, daydreams) or abstract (conjectures, or hallucinations), while others examine the *form* of imagination which is malleable or *plastic* with reference to time (speeds up or slows down), space (opens up or closes in), sensory awareness (heightened or weakened), or causality (logical or irrational).

4.3 Principle: Words Related to Imagination in Different Languages Possess "Family Resemblance"

This acknowledges that words related to imagination range from concrete (e.g., image) to more abstract (e.g., imaginaries), and they can be treated as nouns or as verbs implying action of some kind. While these terms may vary broadly, they share a common meaning that is implicitly understood in a culture. Different groups within the humanities or sciences might favor one of another term that is consistent with how they conceive of the world.

4.4 Principle: Human Sentient Processes are Flexible Adaptations of Primitive Animal Processes

What have we learned from examining the role of imagination in everyday life? As in the case of emotion, we should appreciate the link with other animal species. Both animals and humans have internal (i.e., organic) bodily needs that shape responses to opportunities and constraints or challenges in their surrounding worlds. They must both address novelty and uncertainty in everyday situations. The lower animal species survive by reacting *reflexively* in fixed, instinctual patterns to specific cues. Humans are faced with complex and uncertain situations that demand *interpretation* based on emotionally tinged experiences. Novelty and curiosity work together to stimulate imagination in humans. This gives rise to two underlying themes, *survival* and an *effort after meaning*. The challenge of physical survival requires the clear identification of real threats. There are greater challenges posed by the interpretation of situations and this opens the door for imagination.

4.5 Principle: Imagination Builds the Bridge between Isolation from or Engagement with our Physical and Social Worlds

The "effort after meaning" confronts our isolation within a sentient body of limited duration and a continuous physical and social world. The subjective nature of personal experience can be contrasted with a logical and objective effort to attribute causes to external events. Herein lies the paradox of imagination that, on the one hand, helps us creatively survive in the midst of uncertainty and, on the other hand, preserves emotionalized meanings based on powerful experiences. Teasing these two apart represents the challenge of personal growth and adulthood (sometimes with the assistance of an elder, mentor, or therapist) in contrast with regression and a diffuse sense of self. Common sense is therefore the glue of life.

4.6 Principle: Instrumental and Expressive/Embodied Aspects of Imagination Are complementary

Instrumental imagination is relevant to survival and relates to unanticipated challenges posed by the *disruptions* in physical and social environments and operates through the dialectical interaction of possibilities and constraints. Innovation is predicated on creative solutions given opportunities provided by unexpected challenges. Flexibility in remote associations lies at the heart of this dynamic.

Expressive imagination is tied to personal interpretations of *ambiguous* situations triggering emotionally loaded memories from the past that are unconsciously preserved. While logic is relevant to applying instrumental imagination, conditioning processes link fragments from interpreted situations with emotional reactions.

4.7 Principle: The Contents of Imagination Can Be Understood in Terms of Two Orthogonal Dimensions

Contents encompass all manner of representations (nouns) linking different facets of mainstream and traditional theorizing. These contents include conjectures, illusions, images, imagery, imaginary associations, and so forth. The horizontal dimension is primarily *instrumental*, addressing causes and consequences of disruptions. It contrasts ambiguous *sensations* in situations that lead to *illusions*, and misinterpretations that shape *actions* based on *delusions* or *hallucinations*. The vertical dimension contrasts *sentient mental* dynamics yielding potentially erroneous *conjectures* opposing *organic bodily* processes associated with needs that spontaneously stimulate *fantasies* in accordance with a drive reduction model.

4.8 Principle: Acts of Imagination Can Be Mapped onto Three Dimensions Related to Time, Level of Conscious Awareness, and the Layered Self That Evolves Through Life

The *horizonal* dimension of *time* provides a context within which *acts of imagination* unfold. These include a*mbiguities* in the present, u*ncertainties* about the future, and u*nresolved* emotionally loaded matters from the past. As we try to locate ourselves in the *specious present*, the boundaries between present, past, and future can be porous. It is here that the principle of *suggestion meets connection* is best applied because situations can reawaken *unresolved* memories from the past. The vertical dimension of "levels of awareness" contrasts *conscious attention* in search of explicit meaning in a situation with unconscious or *diffuse awareness* of suppressed or repressed material that manifests in dreams and can influence bodily states and symptoms.

If we pursue an *archeology of the self*, we encounter the stages of intellectual and emotional development described by Piaget and Freud, respectively. This dimension is crucial because a child's interpretation of events can involve spurious correlations, whereas adults with formal operational thinking can apply formal logic to accurately attribute cause. Accordingly, the most interesting of the eight cells formed by this 2 × 2 × 2 design contrast focused attention aimed at the future by an adult mind and diffuse awareness of emotionally loaded early childhood experiences. While formal thinking might solve

Table 2 Levels of imagination.

Transcendent	(Apperceptive; aware of itself)
Instrumental-creative	(Analogy-based)
Expressive-creative	(Metaphor-based)
Imaginary-fantasy	(Motivated based on need)
Imagine	(Purposive, arbitrary construal or novel combination)
Image	(Mere representation in the absence of an object)

instrumental challenges in a logically efficient matter, the poetic expressiveness of the shared life stories, with hidden messages, can lift up empathic listeners.

4.9 Principle: A Hierarchy of Imaginative Processes Range from Syncretic Concrete at the Bottom to Abstract and Symbolic at the Top

When we consider how different scholarly communities address different facets or phases of imagination, a vertical dimension, ranging from concrete (at the bottom) to abstract, puts everything in its logical or metaphorical place (see Table 2).

4.10 Principle: Creative Imagination is Always Emergent and Provides a Way to Resolve Inner Tensions in a Dynamic Way Over Time

Imaginative experiences emerge from the interaction of culture and personal meaning with underlying neural structures and bodily processes. The concept of *Aktualgenese* (Sander, 1930) describes an emerging image that gains clarity over time. Similarly, we can speak of *Gefühlsgenese* as a process whereby emotional experiences emerge as a situation is interpreted more profoundly (Cupchik, 2016). The concept of *Vorstellungsgenese* (Cupchik, 2016) describes how meaningful representations emerge over time motivated by curiosity or the need to reduce inner tension.

4.11 Principle: Meaning is Felt Before Knowing

In accordance with basic ideas from Gestalt psychology and evolutionary principles, meaning is felt before it can be formally articulated. This follows from the ideas to the effect that emotional experiences unfold spontaneously or are triggered by situations. In relation to survival, negative feelings can lead an animal or person to initiate evasive activity, whereas positive feelings can provide a basis for attachment. While an appreciation of deeper meaning can have value, it may be less relevant if the person is dead. Listening to the animal self can provide the sentient self with greater space for breathing (literally) and reflection.

4.12 Principle: Imaginative Representations Have an Aesthetic Quality

They combine subject matter and style or form. In scientific creativity and representational paintings, subject matter and causality are formally defined. The affordances of an image or logic of a causal model make a scene or physical event meaningful because we can assimilate it to existing knowledge. Otherwise, we could not turn on our televisions or laptop computers. In expressive creativity, on the other hand, the transformations or distortions of form related to space, time, texture, and sensory or material quality both express (for the artist) and shape (for the beholder) the very structure of experience.

4.13 Principle: Sensory-Motor and Motor-Sensory Loops Can Be Complementary

Sensory-motor loops refer to a linear process where the discerning of sensory qualities and structures is associated with the performing of well-practiced actions. This dynamic can just as easily be applied to riding a bicycle or driving a car as well as holding a paintbrush to create a particular effect. Motor-sensory loops have the potential to be more creative in the sense that an action can lead to an unexpected effect that has value from the viewpoint of the artist and the actions that led to it can be repeated or iterated so that the entire surface of the unfolding work embodies the quality. This kind of serendipitous process can appear in all creative domains, including art, narratives, dance, and so forth. Once the motor-sensory process is formalized, it can be incorporated in the overall creative act.

4.14 Principle: Creative Imaginative Processes Related to the Natural Sciences and Human Sciences are Complementary

While the humanities have traditionally engaged in an "effort after meaning," science is concerned with the theme of survival. My focus is on a contrast between embodied imagination that expresses our meaningful experiences and instrumental imagination that solves practical problems related to survival. I propose that metaphors underlie expressive imagination and offer novel ways of describing the depth of experiences, whereas instrumental imagination discerns unexpected patterns and analogies that help to solve practical problems by transposing principles from one domain to another.

4.15 Principle: Epistemology Recapitulates Ontology

This is the most challenging of all principles because we take our worlds for granted. Images, knowledge, and beliefs reflect how we conceive of our worlds and what is real in our culture. By implication, acts of imagination and their products will vary across cultures and over time. Accordingly, the beliefs of urban Western industrial societies are fundamentally different from those of indigenous or Eastern cultures that exist in a natural setting. How we understand the world around us is dependent on assumptions that are embedded in the foundations of our minds.

4.16 Principle: Eastern and Western Cultures Reveal Differing Sensitivity to Processes Underlying Imagination

Eastern societies, such as China, are sensitive to the interplay and tensions of a Taoist disposition to be immersed in natural phenomena and a Confucian appreciation of the importance of social and cultural conventions. In a Western context, there is a self-conscious search for patterns, combined with reflections on why events happened in the past and anxious anticipations of the future. The Romantic world-view in Europe represents and attempts to return to Dionysian consciousness that is organic and embedded in nature. Mindfulness training for renewed attention to the present is made all the more important for the Western mind.

5 Conclusions and Implications

The phase theory approach to imagination proposed in this Element is both holistic and grounded in real-world experience and phenomena. Underlying this approach is the concept of "family resemblance" associated with Wittgenstein's assertion in *The Blue Book* regarding "our craving for generality "which is tied to a "tendency to look for something in common to all the entities which we commonly subsume under a general term" (Pompa, 1967, p. 63). Simply put, we assume that a diverse array of words or concepts share in common a unifying theme. In this Element, words like image, imagery, imaginary, reimagine, and so forth are understood to reflect different *phases* or aspects of a more general concept, that of imagination. Exploring the underlying structure of imagination, it was helpful to distinguish between variations that can be associated with contents or nouns, such as image or imagery, and verb forms tied to "acts of imagination," such as imagine or reimagine.

The contents of imagination fit nicely into a linear model whereby sensations lead to actions through the mediating role of the "common sense" that defines the role of imagination (see Figure 1). Problems with the interpreting of ambiguous sensations might give rise to illusions and motor actions can result from misinterpretations of situations which, in extreme cases, lead to hallucinations and subjective experiences projected onto the outside world. Orthogonal to this dimension are conscious thoughts of the sentient mind which can shape conjectures about the meaning of events, contrasted with fantasies associated with bodily and organic needs that work in accordance with a drive reduction model. Acts of imagination were described in three dimensions that took place in time; past, specious present, and future. The acts involved either conscious attention or embodied diffuse awareness and all this is framed by the level of personal development from the syncretic states of the layered self to adult modes of logical inferences. Of course, the most interesting contrast is between actions undertaken by a logical adult mind in planning future adaptive actions that are contrasted with diffuse and unconscious thoughts related to the past that are subject to conditioning, repression, and other psychodynamic processes.

The pragmatics of everyday life lead us to disregard distracting sensations and move immediately to object identification in accordance with needs and goals. Aesthetic activity requires attenuating this rush to judgment so that the qualities and structure of a natural scene or aesthetic work/event can be appreciated. The goal of art and cultural education is to draw our attention to the structure of these sensations. Artists, writers, dancers and other creatives are either naturally disposed and/or trained to be aware of and refine their appreciation of these structures. Aesthetic communication reaches an apex when viewers, readers, and audiences can appreciate the process whereby imaginative acts of creation integrate sensory-motor and motor-sensory actions in the creative process. A dynamic imagination becomes the place, so to speak, where emerging works reside both for creatives and recipients.

We have observed how scholars of different eras, and in faraway places in the world, differ in their accounts of imagination. From a pragmatic Western viewpoint, the person, scientist, or artist stands removed from events and processes in the everyday world. This enables them to "see that" by acting in such and such a manner they are able to foster survival through planned actions. One can also reflect on events and actions in an "effort after meaning" to better understand what has occurred. From the perspective of Taoism in China, the artist or observer is more intimately embedded in natural scenes or depictions of them. This exemplifies a kind of imaginative "seeing as" whereby the event or scene resonates with emotionalized meanings for the artist or viewer. Psychologists of different stripes have focused on either contents or acts of imagination and on different terms and phases of imagination. Cognitive psychologists are more positivist and concrete with their emphasis on concrete images, whereas ego and psychodynamic psychologists favour unconscious and symbolic aspects of fantasy. It bears noting that, in accordance with the richness versus precision tradeoff, phenomena related to imagination have been progressively reduced to (or subsumed within) more general processes so that the essence of imagination in its uniqueness may be lost. In accordance with the grounded approach that underlies my work, it is important to preserve phenomena as events in the world. In a sense, we hold phenomenon in our extended hand while interposing the lenses of theory and method to elucidate underlying processes. We then try to build a bridge between these phenomena and processes in the mind or body that help shape them. In this way, we can merge a "human science" understanding and account of our culturally rich worlds with other levels of causal analysis related to a "natural science" interest in explanation and prediction.

References

Abraham, A. (Ed.). (2020). *The Cambridge handbook of the imagination*. New York: Cambridge University Press.

Arnheim, R. (1954, 1971). *Art and visual perception: A psychology of the creative eye*. Berkeley, CA: University of California Press.

Arnheim, R. (1985). The other Gustav Theodor Fechner. In S. Koch & D. E. Leary (Eds.), *A century of psychology as science* (pp. 856–865). New York: McGraw-Hill.

Ash, M. G. (1998). *Gestalt psychology in German culture, 1890–1967: Holism and the quest for objectivity*. Cambridge: Cambridge University Press. (Original work published 1995)

Baldwin, J. M. (1905). Sketch of the history of psychology. *Psychological Review, 12*(2–3), 144–165.

Baldwin, J. M. (1908). Knowledge and imagination. *Psychological Review, 15* (3), 181–196.

Baldwin, J. M. (1930). James Mark Baldwin. In C. Murchison (Ed.), *A history of psychology in autobiography*, Vol. 1 (pp. 1–30). Worcester, MA: Clark University Press.

Ball, L. J. (2020). Hypothetical thinking. In A. Abraham (Ed.), *The Cambridge handbook of the imagination* (pp. 447–465). New York: Cambridge University Press.

Berlyne, D. E. (1971). *Aesthetics and psychobiology*. New York: Appleton-Century-Crofts.

Boring, E. G. (1950). *A history of experimental psychology*. East Norwalk, CT: Appleton-Century-Crofts. (Original work published 1929)

Boulis, M., Lang, J., Stamatopoulou, D., & Cupchik, G. (2023). Attachment and imagination in Coptic Christians' religious and aesthetic experiences. *Sæculum, 56*, 109–132.

Braun, I. & Cupchik, G. C. (2001). Phenomenological and quantitative analyses of absorption in literary passages. *Empirical Studies of the Arts, 19*(1), 85–109. DOI:10.2190/W6TJ- 4KKB-856F-03VU.

Bullough, E. (1912). "Psychical distance" as a factor in art and an aesthetic principle. *British Journal of Psychology, 1904–1920, 5*(2), 87–118.

Bundy, M. W. (1927). *The theory of imagination in classical and mediaeval thought*. Champaign, IL: University of Ilinois press.

Burwick, F. (1991). *Illusion and the drama: Critical theory of the enlightenment and romantic*. University Park, PA: Penn State University Press.

Burwick, F. & Pape, W. (Eds.). (1990). Aesthetic illusion: Theoretical and historical approaches. Berlin: Walter de Gruyter.

Byrne, R. M. J. (2020). The counterfactual imagination: The impact of alternatives to reality on morality. In A. Abraham (Ed.), *The Cambridge handbook of the imagination* (pp. 447–465). New York: Cambridge University Press.

Carraro, A., Ignacio, A., Cupchik, E. L., & Cupchik, G. C. (2022). The aesthetics of culture. In D. R. Wehrs, S. Nalbantian, & D. M. Tucker (Eds.), *Cultural memory* (pp. 121–136). New York: Routledge.

Cassirer, E. (1950). *The problem of knowledge: Philosophy, science, and history since Hegel*. New Haven, CT: Yale University Press.

Cicero, M. T. (1993). *De Inventione; De Optimo Genere Oratorum; Topica* (H. M. Hubbell, Trans.; Reprint). Cambridge, MA: Harvard University Press. (Original work published 1949)

Cocking, J. M. (1991). *Imagination: A study in the history of ideas* (P. Murray, Ed.). London: Routledge.

Coomaraswamy, A. K. (1974). *The transformation of nature in art*. New Delhi: Munshiram Manoharlal.

Cupchik, G. C. (1995). Emotion in aesthetics: Reactive and reflective models. *Poetics*, *23*, 177–188. DOI:10.1016/0304-422X(94)00014-W.

Cupchik, G. C. (1999). The thinking-I and the being-I in psychology of the arts. *Creativity Research Journal*, *12*(3), 165–173. DOI:10.1207/s15326934crj 1203_1.

Cupchik, G. C. (2011). The digitized self in the internet age. *Psychology of Aesthetics, Creativity, and the Arts*. *5*(4), 318–328. DOI:10.1037/a0024820.

Cupchik, G. C. (2016). *The aesthetics of emotion: Up the down staircase of the mind-body*. Cambridge: Cambridge University Press.

Cupchik, G. C. & Berlyne, D. E. (1979). The perception of collative properties in visual stimuli. *Scandinavian Journal of Psychology*, *20*(1), 93–104.

Cupchik, G., Damasco, V. G., Kiosses, E., et al. (2024). Profiles in pandemic response: Situational helplessness versus coherent resilience. *Canadian Journal of Behavioural Science*. (Feb 8, 2024).

Cupchik, G. C. & Gignac, A. (2007). Layering in art and in aesthetic experience. *Visual Arts Research*, *33*(1), 56–71.

Cupchik, G. C. & Laszlo, J. (1994). The landscape of time in literary reception: Character experience and narrative action. *Cognition and Emotion*, *8*, 297–312. DOI: 10.1080/02699939408408943.

Cupchik, G. C. & Shereck, L. (1998). Generating and receiving contextualized interpretations of sculptures. *Empirical Studies of the Arts*, *16*(2), 179–191. DOI: 10.2190/DR21-Q20D-XNED-VXP8.

Cupchik, G. C., Stamatopoulou, D., & Duan, S. (2021). Finding elusive resonances across cultures and time. In P. Vorderer & C. Klimmt (Eds.), *The Oxford handbook of entertainment theory* (pp. 139–156). New York: Oxford University Press.

Cupchik, G. C., Vartanian, O., Crawley, A., & Mikulis, D. J. (2009). Viewing artworks: Contributions of cognitive control and perceptual facilitation to aesthetic experience. *Brain and Cognition*, *70*(1), 84–91.

Danziger, K. (1990). *Constructing the subject: Historical origins of psychological research*. Cambridge: Cambridge University Press.

Danziger, K. (1997). *Naming the mind: How psychology found its language*. Thousand Oaks, CA: Sage.

Danziger, K. (2000). Making social psychology experimental: A conceptual history, 1920–1970. *Journal of the History of the Behavioral Sciences*, *36*(4), 329–347.

Dewey, J. (1934). *Art as experience*. Oxford: Minton, Balch.

Ehrenzweig, A. (1967). *The hidden order of art: A study in the psychology of artistic imagination*. Oakland, CA: University of California Press.

Ellenberger, H. F. (1970). *The discovery of the unconscious: The history and evolution of dynamic psychiatry*. New York: Basic Books.

Fried, M. (1980). *Absorption and theatricality: Painting and beholder in the age of Diderot*. Berkeley, CA: University of California Press.

Handelman, S. A. (1982). *The slayers of Moses: The emergence of rabbinic interpretation in modern literary theory*. Albany, NY: State University of New York Press.

Hinton, D. (2012). *Hunger mountain: A field guide to mind and landscape*. Boulder, CO: Shambhala.

Hinton, D. (2013). *The four Chinese classics: Tao Te Ching, Chuang Tzu, Analects, Mencius*. Berkeley, CA: Counterpoint.

Hsieh, L. (2015). *The literary mind and the carving of dragons* (V. Y. Shih, Ed.; Revised). The Chinese University of Hong Kong Press/NYRB, New York Review Books.

Hutcheson, F. (2004). *An inquiry into the original of our ideas of beauty and virtue: In two treatises* (W. Leidhold, Ed.). Indianapolis, IN: Liberty Fund. (Original work published 1725).

Ignacio, A. & Cupchik, G. (2020). Understanding fantasy and adult doll play through regression in service of the self. *Imagination, Cognition and Personality*, *40*(3), 290–324.

Irish, M. (2020). On the interaction between episodic and semantic representations – Constructing a unified account of imagination. In A. Abraham (Ed.),

The Cambridge handbook of the imagination (pp. 447–465). New York: Cambridge University Press.

Iser, W. (1978). *The act of reading: A theory of aesthetic response*. Baltimore, MD: Johns Hopkins University Press.

Iser, W. (1993). *The fictive and the imaginary: Charting literary anthropology*. Baltimore, MD: Johns Hopkins University Press.

James, W. (1890). *The principles of psychology, Vol II*. New York Dover. https://doi.org/10.1037/10538-000.

Karnes, M. (2011). *Imagination, meditation, & cognition in the Middle Ages*. Chicago, IL: University of Chicago Press.

Kreitler, H. & Kreitler, S. (1972). *Psychology of the arts*. Durham, NC: Duke University Press.

Kris, E. (1952). *Psychoanalytic explorations in art*. Oxford, UK: International Universities Press.

Law, S. S. (2011). Being in traditional Chinese landscape painting. *Journal of Intercultural Studies*, *32*(4), 369–382.

Lindner, R. W. & Cupchik, G. C. (2024). *Phenoesthetics: Clinical aesthetics and the just noticeable difference*. Tampa, FL: Phenoesthetics.

Lipps, T. (1962). Empathy, inner imitation and sense-feelings. In M. M. Rader (Ed.), *A modern book of esthetics: An anthology* (3rd ed.). New York: Holt, Rinehart, and Winston. (Original work published 1903)

Lyell, C. (1990). *Principles of geology* (M. J. S. Rudwick, Ed.; 1st ed.). Chicago, IL: University of Chicago Press. (Original work published 1830–1833)

Magon, R. & Cupchik, G. (2023). Examining the role of aesthetic experiences in self-realization and self-transcendence: A thematic analysis. *Creativity. Theories – Research – Applications*, *10*(1–2), 68–94.

Mallgrave, H. F. & Ikonomou, E. (Eds.). (1994). *Empathy, form, and space: Problems in German aesthetics, 1873–1893*. Santa Monica, CA: Getty Center for the History of Art and the Humanities.

Mednick, S. A. (1962). The associative basis of the creative process. *Psychological Review, 69*, 220–232.

Mureika, J. R., Dyer, C. C., & Cupchik, G. C. (2005). Multifractal structure in nonrepresentational art. *Physical Review E*, *72*(4), 046101.

Neisser, U. (1967). *Cognitive psychology*. East Norwalk, CT: Appleton-Century-Crofts.

Pfeiffer, K. L. (1990). Fiction: On the fate of a concept between philosophy and literary theory. In F. Burwick & W. Pape (Eds.), *Aesthetic illusion: Theoretical and historical approaches* (pp. 92–104). Berlin: Walter de Gruyter.

Pompa, L. (1967). Family resemblance. *The Philosophical Quarterly*, *17*(66), 63–69.

Poulet, G. (1956). *Studies in human time* (E. Coleman, Trans.). Baltimore, MD: Johns Hopkins University Press. (Original work published 1950)

Rothenberg, A. (1976). Homospatial thinking in creativity. *Archives of General Psychiatry, 33*(1), 17.

Rothenberg, A. (1979). *The emerging goddess: The creative process in art, science, and other fields*. Chicago, IL: University of Chicago Press.

Rothenberg, A. (1980). Visual Art: Homospatial thinking in the creative process. *Leonardo, 13*(1), 17–27.

Rothenberg, A. (1986). Artistic creation as stimulated by superimposed versus combined-composite visual images. *Journal of Personality and Social Psychology, 50*(2), 370–381.

Rothenberg, A. (1988). *The creative process of psychotherapy*. New York: W. W. Norton.

Rothenberg, A. (1990). *Creativity and madness: New findings and old stereotypes*. Baltimore, MD: Johns Hopkins University Press.

Rotter, J. B. (1966). Generalized expectancies for internal versus external control of reinforcement. *Psychological Monographs: General and Applied, 80*(1), 1–28.

Sander, F. (1930). Structure, totality of experience, and Gestalt. In C. Murchison (Ed.), *Psychologies of 1930* (pp. 188–204). Worcester, MA: Clark University Press.

Schiller, F. (1965). *On the aesthetic education of man: In a series of letters* (R. Snell, Trans.). New York: Frederick Ugar. (Original work published 1794)

Schneider, H. J. (1995). The staging of the gaze: Aesthetic illusion and the scene of nature in the eighteenth century. In W. Pape & F. Burwick (Eds.), *Reflecting senses* (pp. 77–95). New York: Walter de Gruyter.

Shanks, M. (2012). *The archaeological Imagination*. Walnut Creek, CA: Left Coast Press.

Sirén, O. (2005). *The Chinese on the art of painting: Texts by the painter-critics, from the 4th through the 19th centuries*. Mineola, NY: Dover. (Original work published 1936)

Stamatopoulou, D. & Cupchik, G. C. (2017). The feeling of the form: Style as dynamic “textured” expression. *Art and Perception, 5*(3), 262–298.

Tateo, L. (2017). Use your imagination: The history of a higher mental function. In B. Wagoner, I. B. de Luna, & S. H. Awad (Eds.), *The psychology of imagination: History, theory, and new research horizon* (pp. 47–66). Charlotte, NC: Information Age.

Vartanian, O. (2020). Imagination in aesthetic experience. In A. Abraham (Ed.), *The Cambridge handbook of the imagination* (pp. 447–465). New York: Cambridge University Press.

Vartanian, O., Cant, J. S., Sama, M. A., et al. (2024, April). *Exploring the neural bases of instrumental vs. expressive imagination: A dynamic functional network connectivity analysis*. Poster presented at the annual meeting of the Society for Neuroscience of Creativity, Toronto, ON.

Werner, H. (1978). On physiognomic modes of perception and their experimental investigation. In S. S. Barten & M. B. Franklin (Eds.), *Developmental processes: Heinz Werner's selected writings*, Vol. 1 (pp. 149–152). New York: International Universities Press.

Werner, H. & Kaplan, B. (1963). *Symbol formation*. Oxford: Wiley.

Wilkinson, E. M. (1945). *Johann Elias Schlegel: A German pioneer in aesthetics*. Oxford: Basil Blackwell.

Winnicott, D. W. (1965). *The maturational processes and the facilitating environment: Studies in the theory of emotional development*. Oxford: International Universities Press.

Winnicott, D. W. (1971). *Playing and reality*. Oxford: Penguin.

Wölfflin, H. (1950). *Principles of art history: The problem of the development of style in later art* (M. D. M. Hottinger, Trans.). Mineola, NY: Dover. (Original work published 1915).

Wulf, C. (2022). *Human beings and their images: Imagination, mimesis, performativity* (E. Hamilton & D. Winter, Trans.). London: Bloomsbury Academic.

Zittoun, T., Glaveanu, V., & Hawlina, H. (2020). A sociocultural perspective on imagination. In A. Abraham, (Ed.), *The Cambridge handbook of the imagination* (pp. 143–161). New York: Cambridge University Press.

Acknowledgements

Many people have contributed directly or indirectly to this Element project. My Research Assistant Clara Rebello has played a crucial role at each stage. The financial support of my Chair in Psychology, Dr. Suzanne Erb, at the University of Toronto, Scarborough is much appreciated. Colleagues and students have contributed in many ways to my research on imagination and emotion. I am thankful for the wise counsel of the distinguished historian of psychology Kurt Danziger. I appreciate the collaborations of my colleagues in Canada, Oshin Vartanian, Jonathan Cant, and Valerie Damasco, as well as colleagues in the United States including Anna Abraham, Don Tucker, Don Wehrs, Michael Shaughnessy, and Robert Lindner. Former students in Canada have played creative roles including Mary Makarious, Zhe Ann Feng, Angelie Ignacio, and Jacob Lang, along with Rayan Magon in India. My European connection encompasses Andrea Carraro (Carraro Lab), Stefania Ballone (Teatro alla Scala) and Yuval Avital in Italy, Ute Ritterfeld, Peter Vorderer, and Gudrun Diermayr in Germany, Chanmi Kim, Thomas van Rompay, and Jeroen van Erp in The Netherlands, with Despina Stamatopoulu in Greece. My collaborators in India include Yashpal and Shubhi Vyas, Ashok Sakdeva, and Meetu Khosla, along with colleagues in China, Xian Zhou, Weiyi Wu, Tingting Wang, Xia Wang, and Siying Duan, as well as Keizo-u Miyasaka in Japan. Many friends from graduate school days and beyond have nourished my imagination, including George Klemp, Susanna Neumann, Bernie Lubell, Krista Phillips, Michael MacConnell, Constance Milbrath, and Oscar Pelta. Closer to home, my parents David Cupchik (1897–1986) and Chana Trifskin (1900–1994) showed the importance of creative humour and insight as a means of addressing the challenging personal history of our family. My wife, Wendy Rosenthall, has been a role model for good judgment in medicine and creativity in fabric arts. My children Eva and David have demonstrated the importance of balancing creativity with kindness. After compiling this list, I realize that imagination is a collective phenomenon so that we all stimulate emotional and intellectual risk-taking in each other, while accepting the challenges posed by personal and cultural histories.

This Element is dedicated to students and colleagues who have expanded my imagination during the past fifty years as a professor at the University of Toronto.

Cambridge Elements

Creativity and Imagination

Anna Abraham
University of Georgia, USA

Anna Abraham, Ph.D. is the E. Paul Torrance Professor at the University of Georgia, USA. Her educational and professional training has been within the disciplines of psychology and neuroscience, and she has worked across a diverse range of academic departments and institutions the world over, all of which have informed her cross-cultural and multidisciplinary focus. She has penned numerous publications including the 2018 book, *The Neuroscience of Creativity* (Cambridge University Press), and 2020 edited volume, *The Cambridge Handbook of the Imagination*. Her latest book is *The Creative Brain: Myths and Truths* (2024, MIT Press).

About the Series

Cambridge Elements in Creativity and Imagination publishes original perspectives and insightful reviews of empirical research, methods, theories, or applications in the vast fields of creativity and the imagination. The series is particularly focused on showcasing novel, necessary and neglected perspectives.

Cambridge Elements

Creativity and Imagination

Elements in the Series

A full series listing is available at: www.cambridge.org/ECAI

www.ingramcontent.com/pod-product-compliance
Ingram Content Group UK Ltd.
Pitfield, Milton Keynes, MK11 3LW, UK
UKHW022144080726
473066UK00010B/742

* 9 7 8 1 0 0 9 4 7 2 0 7 4 *